# Shadow People

# A Journal of the Paranormal

# C.T. Shooting Star

iUniverse, Inc.
New York  Bloomington

# Shadow People
## A Journal of the Paranormal

iUniverse books may be ordered through booksellers or by contacting:

iUniverse
1663 Liberty Drive
Bloomington, IN 47403
www.iuniverse.com
1-800-Authors (1-800-288-4677)

ISBN: 978-1-4401-1565-3 (sc)
ISBN: 978-1-4401-1566-0 (ebook)

Library of Congress Control Number: 2008943550

Printed in the United States of America

iUniverse rev. date: 2/5/2009

*Yea, though I walk through the valley of the shadow of death, I will fear no evil: for thou art with me; thy rod and thy staff they comfort me.*

(Psalm 23:4)

# Contents

# Foreword

You might be surprised to know that I never totally believed in ghosts until I was fifty years of age. Perhaps I would have learned more about my fear of the unknown, if I had been more open-minded.

In my young and foolish days, I found myself stranded in a small desolate western town waiting until the morning for the bus to take me to the next place. I walked out to the end of the track, away from prying eyes until I found a nice bed of long, dry grass close to the side of a narrow road where I settled down and watched the cool prairie wind blow the field tops in gentle waves.

I was relaxed and I thought that everything was fine, until I noticed the cemetery. In my imagination, I felt the urge to escape from the grasps of dried out husks of straw hands.

But before the thought of moving away from the cemetery was firmly planted in my mind, I noticed the two headlights coming slowly down the road towards me. I slid back down an embankment and hid low in the grass. Relieved that the patrol car had passed me by without incident, I began to relax again; however, sleep eluded me. I shall never forget the eeriness of that graveyard.

$$* \quad * \quad *$$

My first encounter with the unknown started after I met a family that had spent many sleepless nights in their home because of ghostly beings. They were just amazing people. Each family member was like a soldier, who put up with ongoing harassment from the enemy. Going crazy wasn't an option and going public was considered the next best thing to going crazy.

The decision to publish all of their ghostly accounts was made because the narrator, along with his wife Cathy and their young two children, wanted people to know about the existence of negative entities and how to take appropriate action against them.

Originally, it was the narrator's ghostly allies who suggested that he publish the techniques which work best against negative entities, even if the reader was not yet ready to believe in the spirit world. The narrator decided that after he had dealt with all of his own paranormal difficulties first; then he would do what his ghostly allies suggested. Now, the narrator is ready to tell the rest of the story.

For psychics and non-psychics alike, this detained account of spirit harassment is aimed at people who need to remove unwanted entities, elementals and other energies from their living spaces, in addition to increasing their understanding of paranormal phenomena.

Yours truly,
R.G. Hilson
November 2008

P.S. Due to an increase in reported cases of malicious shadow entities, sometimes known as "the shadow people," the narrator has provided a blueprint for those who need a "quick fix" protection plan (see part three). The blueprint blends some simple, quick fix remedies and ULF strategies for those who have ongoing paranormal problems at home.

P.P.S. The names have been changed to protect the innocent. It should also be noted that all members of the family are psychically sensitive, except for the narrator.

# Acknowledgements

I was fortunate to have divine intervention before I was able to cope with my adversaries "on my own." The Senior Council (or the Senior Council of Elders), contacted me and told me that the Angel of Truth would monitor my affairs and advise me.

I would like to thank the Council again for their kindness; the Angel of Truth for his friendship; all the angels who supported us; in addition to our guardians for their continuing assistance.

# Part One

## The Night Side of Nature

*Many people today have lost faith because they think that the all powerful being that put them here in the first place has forsaken them. Nothing could be further from the truth. The old souls amongst us chose to learn the lessons of the negative worlds, before they would reside in the positive ones. This book contains all of the lessons which were learned.*

Most of the supernatural incidents recorded in this account occurred during 2007 and continued throughout 2008, until the fall. (At that point, I decided to draw the noose and establish a more effective household energy shield).

The main reason for the personal harassment was because I was preparing this project on how to eliminate intruding spirits. Believe me, the harassing spirits knew what I was doing and they didn't like it. The closer I got to the truth it seemed, the worse the harassment.

The continual harassment meant that I would have to follow the path of shadows until I discovered all the answers which I sought, before I would be able to come up with some viable solutions. In other words, staying on the path and seeing it through until the end was my only real option.

*   *   *

*I don't think we should be totally dismissive of other worlds which might resemble Hell, since there are powerful spirits with evil intentions who dwell in these places and on our plane.*

In a book called "The Doorway," a soldier spirit spoke about a place which was in between the higher places of Heaven and the Earth plane. The soldier did not see angels with wings or harps there; but the soldier spirit did mention that he had knowledge of some spirits, who were so degraded that they had to be reabsorbed into the life-essence. This so called cosmic melting-pot is called the second death; since the entity ceases to exist as an individual. Entities who attach themselves to mortals for the sole purpose of committing evil acts are candidates for the second death.

Besides the spirits who attach themselves to mortals, there are spirits that come from places which are diametrically opposed to the heavenly realms. The spirits from these places roam the Earth plane and cause problems, until they are challenged. I was told that all of our difficulties in our previous home were caused by a spirit from such a place. Some people might face other life changing challenges, but I believe that there is nothing more life changing than a powerful evil spirit that wants to destroy you. By the way, I'm not advocating that you go and look for a worthy opponent in order to test your capabilities as a light warrior. Just trust in the wisdom of the universe, if you find yourself in the same situation as I did.

I admit that my situation was very extreme. The Council of Elders intervened on my behalf. They gave me a choice. They would try and convert this powerful spirit to the good side, so that the spirit could make restitution; or the spirit could be imprisoned instead. I agreed that the spirit should make amends through restitution, but the mission failed and the spirit was imprisoned on my premises.

There were no further problems for over a year and I thought it was over. However, three powerful spirits took the place of the imprisoned one and they released him as well. My adversary continued to plot against me while I dealt with his army. Eventually, he taught his followers how to use telepathy.

Thankfully, this sudden escalation of events also came to the attention of the Council. My adversary was sentenced and imprisoned by order of the Council, in a more secure setting this time. The important point here is that divine justice does take place, whether we are aware of it or not.

# 1.0 The path of shadows

*Many spirits walk the path of shadows; so you need to be prepared to deal with a variety of situations.*

Shadow entities have the ability to materialize and take on the identities of those whom you know. The following lesson is taken from the book Ghostly Allies:

> There are many things which give them away. Impish looks or expressions which don't fit are one of the giveaways. Entities can also superimpose over people, so that the voices you think you hear are the people you are talking with. If you should ever come in contact with these mischievous spirits, you will be extremely impressed with their power and ingenuity. Regardless of your curiosity level, you must be prepared to eliminate them without hesitation, since they can be relentless in trying to undermine you, when you least expect it.

John-Roger in his book "Psychic Protection" wrote about "forms" that were never human and could masquerade as highly evolved spiritual beings. Also, author Joe Fisher investigated channeling and wrote a book called "The Siren Call of Hungry Ghosts." He was introduced to knowledgeable or familiar spirits, who manipulated and lead the gullible down the proverbial garden path. One could easily conclude from his book and several other investigative studies that there are different levels of human and non-human spirits on our Earth plane.

Brad Steiger in his book "Real Ghosts, Restless Spirits and Haunted Places" differentiates between a lost soul and a spirit parasite. The spirit parasite is capable of possessing and manipulating the host much like a lost soul. Steiger claims that he has encountered spirit parasites in places of violence which he described as "hideous and grotesque in appearance," often with reptilian-like features.

I have taken digital pictures of human faces with reptilian features in historical forts. Although I wasn't intimidated by the soldiers' masquerade, I can appreciate why people of the past might have considered these specters in the timbers and on the walls to be evil demons from Hell. As they say, don't get hung up on appearances.

On the other hand, the story of the Hilltop demon really did hit a nerve with me. The demon was featured in the non-fiction book, the "Black Hope Horror" which took place in Texas during the early 1980's. The book was written by Ben and Jean Williams, along with John Shoemaker. It was published by William Morrow Inc. in 1991. The book was also made into a television movie called Grave Secrets: The legacy of Hilltop Drive which starred Patty Duke, David Selby and David Soul.

I had been in touch with the spirit world a few years ago and I was told that Black Hope Horror story was based on a true account. This very angry, snake like demon had the power to trap and enslave spirits. There were spirits who had been enslaved as a result of the demon conflicts which had occurred in my previous home also. Even though they were personally pleading for me to "Free the Slaves," Adam told me that it would be okay. He reminded me that the Creator was aware of the situation and that He would set them free when it was time. I simply had to have faith.

Dr. Scott Peck in his book: "People of the Lie" claimed to have come face to face with the Evil One through a case of possession. Again the entity which claimed to be the Evil One was a reptilian, snake like spirit. Peck reminds us that the only power that evil has over us is through our human belief. In other words, the only way for evil to destroy goodness is through lies. In fact, my favourite spiritual maxim from Padre Pio: The Stigmatist is: "The lie is the child of the demon." Dr. Peck also reminds us that the most vulnerable people in our society are those who are lonely, since they are more easily confused and taken to a higher level of despair in one fatal swoop, after listening to a multitude of lies.

\*   \*   \*

The Roman Catholic Church decreed that a case of diabolic possession which took place in Earling, Iowa in 1928 was authentic. Satan spoke directly to Father Riesinger, who performed the exorcism. The Evil One stated that the whole issue of possession began before time itself and in accordance with a set of strict laws.

In the beginning that might have been true; but is it possible that the great teacher who was sent to Earth to teach humans how to deal with negativity became the most negative thing on Earth? In the long run that will make us stronger yet, if we adopt the higher principles and the universal light force more often, both individually and collectively.

Yes, I realize that most contemporary psychics today find it fashionable to humbug the idea of a satanic figure which they claim is based on the teachings of the church. When you add the notion of Satan as nothing more than a fear mongering tactic, then it becomes even easier to dismiss the devil as a phony. But how much of a problem is the hierarchy of evil on this planet? On this point the reader must form their own judgment, according to their own beliefs.

# 1.1 Shadow people

We have seen shadow people in the same way that most reports have described them:

- Cathy, Adam and Jacob have all seen "human shaped shadow people" at home, in the reverse firing chamber at Fort Henry, in addition to the tunnels which surround Fort Niagara.
- The boys have both witnessed the "hat man" type of shadow person as well.
- I have personally witnessed the "black mist shadow person" version.
- The notorious "red-eyed shadow person" was common enough at our home, at one time. This particular version says a great deal about what the shadow people are all about.

## What do these shadow creatures really want?

We believe that the modus operandi of the shadow people is to instill fear in us, so they can gain power from that emotion. For example, if you observe them and they disappear; then that uncertainty creates a sense of unease.

Their favourite trick is to stand right behind you with their burning red eyes glaring through the back of your skull. Someone who is psychic can actually sense their red eyes staring at them from behind. If you turn around fast enough, you will see them, just before they disappear.

The real nasty aspect of these creatures is that they have the potential to gain energy from your distress while you are asleep. Sometimes people wake up in the middle of the night because they feel like someone is trying to choke them. In some cases, shadow people are responsible for this so called "choking sensation."

In brief, these beings are energy vampires and not of the light.

## There are at least three "types" of shadow people

We consider shadow people to be demons, poltergeists and "low level" evil spirits. Most shadow people are "de-grades" who do not cause problems for the most part. These "low level" evil spirits don't have enough power to move a tissue across a kitchen counter top. Nevertheless, they wish they could in order to cause problems. So they join together whenever it is possible and create a poltergeist. Fortunately, a poltergeist created from these so called "de-grades" is a fairly weak one and it is not really a serious threat.

The second type of "shadow person" is a copy. The shadow is not an individual entity at all; it's a decoy. Powerful entities can create shadows to protect themselves in situations in which they could get into difficulties with positive forces. They can also use their own "shadow being" to blend in with other shadows as a defensive strategy.

For example, there was a seven foot shadow person who decided to walk through our home, the day that I had finished working on my manuscript "Lessons from the Heavenly Council." That being was a shadow only. The actual demon would not have been so brazen.

The shadow people with the glowing red eyes create the most fear. This strategy also makes them the most powerful group. They are also responsible for the second group of shadow people (i.e., the copies).

In summary:

- demons prefer their shadow form because it doesn't require a lot of power and it's a fairly safe mode to operate in
- shadow people thrive on negativity; so their only mission is to create more negativity and feed on it

Another interesting point about these creatures is that most of them appear to be male figures; but perhaps that will change over time.

# 1.2 Poltergeists

The term poltergeist was introduced to England and possibly the English language when Catherine Crowe published her classic tale "The Night Side of Nature" (London, 1848).

A century later, Harry Price claimed that he had enough cases of documented poltergeist activity to fill several volumes. He perceived a poltergeist to be "an alleged ghost, elemental, entity, agency, secondary personality, "intelligence," "power," spirit, imp, or "familiar," with certain unpleasant characteristics" (Price, 1945, p. 1).

He also described the modus operandi of poltergeist activity from other places and other ages:

> According to the many reports of its activities, in all lands and in all ages, the Poltergeist is mischievous, destructive, noisy, cruel, erratic, thievish, demonstrative, purposeless, cunning, unhelpful, malicious, audacious, teasing, ill-disposed, spiteful, ruthless, resourceful and vampiric. A ghost haunts; a Poltergeist infests. A ghost likes solitude; a Poltergeist prefers company. A ghost seeks the half-light; a Poltergeist will "perform" in sunlight (Ibid., 1945, p. 1).

Catherine Bowman in her psychic protection book: "Entities Among Us," thought that poltergeists were evil spirits. In addition, she claimed that a poltergeist could either be a "coagulation of negative thought forms or a group of angry spirits joined together" (Bowman, 2003, p. 61).

I would add one more important detail to Bowman's definition. The main reason that angry spirits join together in the first place is to gain more power than they would have otherwise.

In addition, all historical accounts show that a poltergeist attack can be a shocking experience for the unwary. I've had many such experiences myself.

# Poltergeist attack

*The poltergeist strategy of like-minded spirits banding together was implemented in the following case because they needed the extra power to maximize their terror tactics.*

I was working on my manuscript in the basement one evening during the summer of 2008. I placed my large Webster's dictionary on the bookshelf behind the computer monitor; but it was promptly pushed back out towards me. Then it literally flew off the shelf and hit the table beside my desk. At the same time my keyboard flew out at me and the cat's scratching tower was knocked over. I could both hear and sense the keyboard move and I saw the cat tower go over. The tower had a square base and each side was a foot long. I've never seen the one in the basement knocked over before. It was like a wave of energy or several spirits working in unison and doing everything at the exact same time.

I jumped into action immediately. I had the crystal power rod in my hand within seconds, since it was situated below my mouse pad drawer. Then I grabbed the tomahawk from one of my barrister bookcases. Both of the power rods were kept close together for obvious reasons.

I ran upside and asked Cathy if everything was okay. She claimed that she had become extremely dizzy, about a minute before which was the same time that the poltergeist struck. Apparently, the energy transference from the poltergeist had circulated upstairs to Cathy.

I requested extra power for our home and I waved the power rods around. Cathy's hands were still cold, but she was beginning to warm up. That was before we went upstairs to the second story. It was cold up there because a spirit had decided to stand as close to Cathy as possible. Instead of the tingly feeling which she usually gets when our spirit allies are around, she kept getting a cold feeling. She was also complaining that whenever I waved the tomahawk near her, it was sending off too much energy. She asked me to stand beside her instead. I did that and kept up with the action. Then we went into her office. Whatever was following her kept moving around. It created a cold spot from one place to the next. Adam could track the spirit as well.

I decided to supercharge the tomahawk. I positioned the crystal power rod in a vertical placement, so that the blunt end was touching the tomahawk's handle. After I hit ever cold spot imaginable, I stopped. I told them that a guardian was present and the poltergeist had been removed. Adam agreed with me. He said that the poltergeist had been extremely angry about my writing, but it was over.

Fortunately, my quick action in the basement had eliminated the poltergeist almost immediately. Apparently all of the cold spots upstairs were related to positive energy. The extra positive energy was also one of the reasons that Cathy had been complaining about the power rods. Nevertheless, I'm sure our helpful guardian didn't mind the positive energy from the power rods.

# The force

*The second story is called the "force." Poltergeists are often referred to as evil spirits. Nevertheless, the term evil does not have the same meaning in the spirit world as it does in our world. Evil is actually an unfortunate term in that humans have both good and evil in them. Perhaps that is why it's preferable to use the term "negative" when describing most spirits. Nevertheless,"the force" in this story fed on negative energy from humans and it was evil.*

A negative power called the force rivaled the demons from our other home in terms of malicious intent. The force was like a supercharged version of a poltergeist. In fact, it was the most powerful adversary that we needed to defeat in our second home. Hopefully, you will never have to deal with such an unbelievable situation. This is the complete story of the force.

There didn't seem to be a clear beginning to this problem, but the first time we were able to identify this new phenomenon was on Sunday

November 26, 2006. Several cats had been locked up in various rooms for the night. Adam had his closet door wrenched from its moorings and pushed out at him. A new vacuum handle had been taken apart and destroyed. The entire head; plus the handle had to be replaced. I went around the house earlier in the week, hoping that I had taken care of the problem before we had another crisis. Instead, I was called upstairs to investigate another mysterious incident.

Jacob had been arguing with us over school work this past week. Adam had snapped a few times as well. After speaking with Adam, we knew beyond a doubt that there was another evil spirit in our home. Adam said that Jacob had been feeding it with his negative behaviour; since he appeared to be the weakest link. Adam wanted to present his proof to Cathy; so I followed both Adam and Cathy downstairs to the kitchen area. We were standing in the kitchen area discussing all of the unexplained things which had gone wrong this week, when Cathy said that we must all be happy to get rid of the evilness.

At that point, something totally malignant and ominous came into the room. Adam agreed with me later that it was out of a Hollywood horror movie. The evil force punched Adam and attacked Cathy. She bent over in pain with a contorted face. Her head was reeling and she could barely catch her breath. In the meanwhile, I had my power rod with me; so I trained it directly on her. Whatever had attacked her was very powerful and very evil. The force backed off because of the crystal rod. Adam said that the evil force knew enough to hide when the power rod was around. It was so powerful that the rod only slowed it down. It would have to be captured in a hiding spot. Cathy added that this particular event was going to be a learning experience for us. It was special.

I spoke to Adam on the upstairs steps a few minutes later about the nature of evil. He said that the evil force had been created by negative entities in our outside environment. The force had gained access through our force field because something negative happened inside our own home. Negative forces are fed by negative human energies. In general, they go from house to house; but they sometimes feed off a household, until the people put their home up for sale. In our case, the force noted that we were quite a challenge; so it decided to stay.

Both Adam and Jacob described it as "pure evil" which was fed by human beings.

I asked Adam, "How can you control pure evil?"

He sounded like a sage of old when he said, "By living the Ten Commandments. The opposite of the Ten Commandments will feed evil."

I asked him again if he could tell me about the nature of true evil.

He replied, "You can never understand the true nature of evil because if you do, it will seek you out and destroy you. Humans have both evil and good in them."

According to Adam, the Creator is all loving and merciful. Only an all powerful being could create a world which balances all aspects of good and evil. Remember, the old souls amongst us chose to learn lessons in the negative worlds, before they would reside in the positive worlds.

Now I was anxious to lay into this thing. I asked Jacob for help. He knew the hiding places. Because I used the tomahawk to attack the force, I ended up splitting it in two. Jacob came to the rescue and removed one half of it. Cathy was preparing the house for a visit and she began to sing. Her song invited the good spirits into the house long enough to remove the other half of the evil force without the use of a power rod this time. In our previous home, this would not have been possible.

From this point on, we would have to be careful about managing anger; since evil energies make people do evil things. Then the energies feed off anger like energy vampires.

The next time we encountered the force, it was twelve o'clock midnight on Saturday April 28, 2007. I was on the second level of our home and I had just come out of the master bedroom with my two power rods, when I saw Cathy doubled over at the top of the stairs. She said that she had been punched. I called for the white light to fill the house. The house changed from negative to positive immediately. Nevertheless, the force was only wounded and had hatred and revenge on its mind.

Within five minutes, we could smell candles. Cathy could also tell that there was going to be trouble. Almost on cue, the air was "sucked out of the house." Everyone appeared to be vulnerable to this psychic phenomenon except for me. Cathy felt cold and faint, as I instructed her and the boys to open the front door and let in the cool night air. In the meantime, I asked for the white light again. Unfortunately, for us, this was not the end of it. About two weeks later, it started again.

On May 13, 2007 Adam was playing his portable electric organ and the plug was pulled. I challenged the entity to come to me. Oddly enough, a wooden peg from the wall mounted coat rack in our previous home was dropped in front of me instead. I thought that I had defeated the spirit, but I was wrong. It appeared to be a fear tactic.

Cathy forgot to mention to me that she had been walking up the street with the boys earlier in the day, when she ran into something evil. She couldn't breathe very well; but she was able to make her way back home. She said that whatever had attacked her had come into the house with her. There had been a smell afterwards and Adam's portable organ plug had been pulled out. The force appeared to have a pet peeve with Adam and his music.

Both Adam and Cathy reminded me what we were up against. This large, potent force went into homes and sucked up all the negative energy it could find. Sometimes it would just cause trouble; then it would retreat back to the street.

Cathy said that I had not defeated it. She described the evil force as being similar to a poltergeist, but worse. In brief, a poltergeist can be several ghosts or elementals which join together, or it can be created by humans.

At first, Adam actually questioned whether I could defeat it. It had stood up to me and taunted me. Then Adam came up with the answer. He said that the power rods and the jet dragon could defeat it. But the force would only stay long enough to make its point and then it would leave for greener pastures. Nevertheless, the force was trying to be a hero. My plan was to capture it in due course.

The force finally attacked again. Fortunately, Cathy's arms had begun to tingle about the same time. The tingling was a sign that our ghostly allies were just a wee bit concerned. I'm sure they stepped in to prevent the problem from escalating.

This force was smart because it chose Jacob as its first target. It used him like a puppet. Jacob started an argument with me for no reason.

I simply left the room to avoid the confrontation. My committee had to deal with the problem and protect Cathy at the same time. Afterwards, Adam told me that the evil force had taken over Jacob. His eyes showed the possession. However, the spirit was not able to possess him that long. But if I had gotten involved, it could have been worse. Sometimes, it's better to walk away.

May 20, 2007

The force always attacked us on the Sabbath for some reason. Our next encounter on the Sabbath started when Cathy noticed a smell on the ground floor. By the time I had retrieved the power rods from the basement, Jacob was complaining about "the smell" upstairs. I darted up the stairs and I walked right into it, at the top of the staircase. I continued with my attack because both Cathy and Jacob were concerned about the air being "sucked up" again. Pure evil cannot be totally contained; it appears to have certain vampire tendencies which help it to sustain itself. This pure evil force was wounded; but it would still be difficult to destroy, according to Jacob.

I whirled the crystal power rod at the heavens. At the same time, I asked for the white light to flood our home. I also wanted all entity intruders removed from our home. I did this twice. Then I re-directed the power rod at anything left standing in the house.

Cathy noticed an immediate improvement in the house. She stated that the force was now either lying low or it had left. There was no further sign of it that evening, so I expect that it was put off for the time being; however, this powerful evil force was still in the neighbourhood and there was a good chance that it would want revenge.

May 26, 2007

We came under attack a day earlier than expected. Adam asked me to come upstairs quickly with the power rod. Adam and Cathy both agreed that it was right out of the classic ghost film: "The Uninvited." Everyone could smell "the problem." Then it disappeared just as fast.

Adam had been upstairs playing his portable organ. He was in a joyful mood and he had no troubles on his mind. He was playing the instrument very softly. His intention was to continue with the delightful melody, as there was no other influence to make him do otherwise. According to his account, he couldn't help it when the music began to sound sad. Then he started to hit the keys in an aggressive manner. The resulting music was distasteful. Cathy got upset with him and told him to stop playing. Adam became angry and pushed the chair over. Then he went downstairs to the living room and started to shout, until he realized that there must be a problem in the house. That's when he called me.

Cathy, Adam and Jacob were all taken back by this event. All three of them agreed that the events were similar to the piano scene in "The Uninvited" in which the music changed from happy to sad. Alan also stated that the force had tried to possess him.

Man is only just beginning to understand the power of music and how evil spirits can influence us through it. Adam told me that music is a powerful agent for both good and evil. Perhaps too much emphasis has been placed on other aspects of violence in the media and perhaps not enough on demonic music. My advice is that anyone who gets angry listening to music should stop listening to it immediately.

I decided that I would need a full debriefing with Jacob because of the seriousness of the event. I started off by asking Jacob about pure evil again. Jacob explained that pure evil can be found in other parts of the universe. But most of the pure evil we experience in our world is caused by man. Man has an evil side to him and he creates evil.

Evil spirits can also change a harmonious environment, to one of negativity. According to Jacob, when a good home turns bad, it's often because of the negative energies in the environment. If you lack a sense of awareness, it's easy to overreact to something unknown. Some people simply move away or they divorce without understanding what really started the problem in the first place.

I tried to understand the significance of what Jacob was saying and I was determined to get at the heart of evil; so I continued with our debriefing session. I sat on the floor while Jacob stood and explained. It was late on Saturday night. Both Cathy and Adam were upstairs on the computer and I knew I would get the information which I required.

Jacob explained that there are basically three worlds which we deal directly with. The first one is the fourth dimension which is the spirit world; the second one is Hell which may be a difficult concept for some people to appreciate and the third one is our world. Jacob explained that pure evil often comes through a crack between our world and another place. The crack can be large depending on the amount of negativity in the environment. The crack itself is a bit different from a portal as well.

The evil force which attacked us was an energy vampire. It fed on emotions. Because it had a shell (or a force field), it was difficult to eliminate. At first, I thought it was so powerful and so evil that I would not be able to eliminate it. It kept coming back to cause problems even when I weakened its negative force field with the power rods. I even hit it from behind with the tomahawk when its force field was down one time. However, the real reason the force left after a confrontation was because it was intelligent enough to know that it could not survive a sustained attack with two power rods.

Jacob was concerned that this particular negative power was camouflaged. Even those who can see ghosts would probably not see it. If I had aimed lower towards the ground, I would have finished it. Unfortunately, I didn't know that it had dropped to the ground once it was hit. It stayed low and drifted out. Jacob added that I might get it the next time, if it decided to return. My ghostly allies would help if necessary; but they considered this one to be a challenge for me alone.

Jacob also mentioned that the crack had pulled the force back into it. The force was badly wounded and the crack itself contained power which the force needed. Jacob also thought that the crack might have a limited amount of power. He felt that the crack would fail at some future time, if the force was wounded enough times. That might have been be wishful thinking; but Jacob made sense most of the time. From my perspective, I was not willing to wait for the crack to disappear. The sooner I eliminated the problem, the better.

Jacob also mentioned Hell in his conversation with me. Those who are really evil and commit murders without regard for others, go straight to Hell. There are probably millions of souls there. Those who have committed crimes or major wrongs can still be allowed into Heaven, if they perform some worthy deeds. You can be "punished" and still get into Heaven in other words.

After Jacob said this, he stated that Adam would be calling for him. Within five seconds, Adam opened an upstairs door and called downstairs for Jacob to come up.

I asked Jacob, "How did you know that Adam would call for you."

Jacob replied," I just know."

July 20, 2007

We were getting ready for bed when I noticed the distinct smell of an evil spirit. I retrieved the crystal rod from the basement and returned. However, by then the situation had developed into a major problem, so I had to go back for the tomahawk as well. The whole downstairs had become a stench of unbelievable proportions. Cathy had to get away from it because she was overcome. It was so bad that I had to ask for more light, about six or seven times.

As I was going around the house, with the power rods, Jacob shouted out that he had been attacked as well. The force had just left his room. He told me to come up to his room and to hang around for a little while. Sure enough, the force returned and I was waiting for it with both of the power rods and all the power of the universe which I could muster.

Jacob told me later that the whole thing was well planned for this late hour. The force was counting on the element of surprise in order to test our limits. Nevertheless, it had under-estimated our reserve power and the attack ended up being a suicide mission.

# 1.3 The earthbound

*When most people think of ghosts or discarnate beings, they think of the earthbound. The classic writings of Carl A. Wickland, M.D. provide us with a good place to start.*

Anyone who has read "Thirty years among the dead," by Carl A. Wickland, M.D. will appreciate that obsessed spirits have no supernormal knowledge. These spirits are often the ones who attach themselves to the living and create a lot of misery for both themselves and their hosts. Moreover, many spirits of the dead which Dr. Wickland dealt with were not able to detach themselves from the people, places and things of the material world without help from other spirits and Dr. Wickland. Thus, they were not able to progress to the light of a higher dimension. Because of their limited beliefs or obsessions, the higher dimension would stay closed to them until they were educated enough to realize that it was their own limited views which made them earthbound.

Dr. Wickland also believed that some spirits were so brainwashed or obsessed that they couldn't be helped by mortals. In this category, one would expect to find obsessed spirits who were subjected to the spreading of falsehoods. Because these spirits believed the lies they were told, they became earthbound in their own self-created, private hell.

One case in Dr. Wickland's book was about a leader of a Christian movement who taught false doctrines. Her case is a warning to others to tell the truth about spiritual matters, as opposed to spreading dogma. According to Dr. Wickland, anyone who preaches the wrong message will probably end up with those of the same mind set in the after life.

One of Dr. Wickland's most famous spirit contacts was Madam Blavatsky. Madam Blavatsky wrote and lectured about reincarnation when she was alive, but she changed her mind after going to the other side. She stated that memories of "past lives" are caused by spirits who impress their own memories on the living. Many people then think that they are reliving their past. In fact, Madam Blavatsky is correct in that spirits do implant images of their past life on the living. *(Note: Refer to 5.4 for further information)*.

However, believing in spirit implanted images does not discount reincarnation. Some of the followers of Madam Blavatsky only understood or believed in certain elements of reincarnation. As a result, some of her flock attached themselves to children. With so many of her followers being earthbound, she probably felt the pressure to change her mind about the whole idea of reincarnation much like throwing the baby out with the bathwater. Unfortunately, it would be her job to educate those whom she instructed during her mortal existence, so they could reach a higher level of understanding; in order to see a higher dimension. Then she would be allowed to proceed herself.

In brief, no matter how popular a psychic is; or convincing a spiritual leader's arguments appear to be; you should only adhere to the "so called truths" that resonate with you.

# The problem of the earthbound

Dr. Wickland states that discarnate intelligences are consciously or unconsciously, attracted to the magnetic light of mortals. Once a spirit attaches itself to the magnetic field of the aura of a living human being, they have the potential to influence, obsess or possess that human being. In other words, a spirit can influence a susceptible sensitive person with its thoughts and its emotions. A spirit can also weaken a susceptible person's will power and even control their actions. For the host, this may mean a great deal of distress and mental confusion.

According to Dr. Wickland, people who are most vulnerable to spirit attachments are those with health concerns and addictions; and the criminal minded who are predisposed to negative influences. Wickland states that in our past, obsessed spirits have been the by-product of human selfishness and false teachings, thrust blindly into a spirit existence and held there in bondage because of ignorance. As such, the influence of discarnate entities has become one of the leading causes of many of the inexplicable and obscure events of Earth life and a large part of the world's misery.

# 1.4 Psychical phenomena

*Some interesting psychical phenomena occurred, during the time we were in conflict with the shadow entities. Two examples of this type of activity are: "Our ghost cat" and "Our ghostly doubles."*

## Our ghost cat

There had been several sightings of a ghostly black cat in our previous home. Recently, another black cat, or the same one had been seen going into Jacob's room and disappearing. Adam also saw the mysterious cat go around several corners. Whenever he followed it; it disappeared.

Often our four cats would scratch at the master bedroom door. This usually indicated that a cat was locked up. After opening the closet door and allowing the cats to look inside; they would stop scratching.

Cathy also saw the ghost cat seemingly jump towards her one time. She put her arms up to protect herself. But again, the spirit disappeared.

The first time I saw the ghost cat in our new home, it bumped my mouse pad drawer with a bang. The drawer actually *moved.* I saw the black tail of the cat underneath the drawer. I also *saw* the animal's tail go around the corner. There was no where for an animal to hide. It's always a shock to see something disappear when you know what you saw *was what you saw.*

One morning I heard a mournful cat's meowing. I didn't recognize the cat's cry. Later that same day, I was petting Sheba our female black cat. I felt another cat brush up against me. It felt the same as Sheba. No other cat did what she was capable of doing. She was very dainty. She always stood on her hind legs and gave me a good brushing as she came up. Then she liked to dive down. As I turned, I saw the same black tail; but there was no cat in sight. As I stood up in wonderment, our male black cat was calmly resting up on the kitchen counter. Tommy was not that quick and there was no way he could have disappeared and ended up on the countertop with my quick reflexes. Moreover, none of our cats would have bumped me from behind in a sitting position and then just taken off. Regardless, I had my eyes on the tail and *there was no cat.*

Adam and Jacob were playing their instruments upstairs. Jacob was on bass guitar when a cat jumped over the amp and brushed up against his pant leg. But when he looked down; there was no cat to be seen anywhere.

After our trip to Fort Malden and the Battlefield of the Thames, the black cat struck again. We had been home for about fifteen minutes and I was checking the back seat of the car for luggage. I was on the driver side of the car and Jacob was standing by the other side of the car. Both outside lights were on and we could see very clearly. Jacob had just taken the last item from the back car seat. He claimed he saw a shadow stir and then a large cat figure jumped out at him. It was the same cat which had been haunting our home. I was rather disappointed because I had both seen and felt the phantom cat several times before. But this time, I saw nothing. On the other hand, Jacob was very startled. He was put off by the event because he thought that the ghost was coming right at him.

* * *

Finally, World War III broke out one night, after we had gone to bed. The most horrendous cat shrieks woke us up. Cathy dashed out into the hallway, only to find a few contented cats at peace, enjoying the nightlife. All of our cats were accounted for and there were no bad feelings between them. The warrior cats did not belong to our world.

Things didn't settle down after the first night either. I was woken up several times by the sound of a "cat fight." The screeching was always high end and it always sounded like an animal was being clawed rather badly. The sound of the fight was so eerie that I couldn't get it out of my mind. The worse aspect of it was that it seemed to be a repeat of the same battle. Another curious thing was that the battle always stopped when you got up to investigate. In this way, the cat phenomenon was identical to the phantom pipes and fifes music that we had in the house, on prior occasions.

There was also some speculation that we might have had more than one phantom cat around; however, all sightings of the phantom black cat were similar in nature. If there was only one phantom cat, then perhaps the phantom cat was keeping other phantom cats away from the house; or perhaps the phantom cat was trying to show us how its life ended on Earth. That would put us in the same camp as the owners of the haunted house at Cliff's End, in the 1944 ghost film "The Uninvited." In the film, one of the two ghosts in the haunted house, always cried in the middle of the night until her problem was dealt with. I prefer the first interpretation for the time being. The phantom cat fights seem a bit too sporadic for a re-enactment event. Moreover, I believe our phantom cat liked humans and wanted to be part of our family.

After a few more blood curdling phantom cat fights, I stopped getting up in the middle of the night becuase I knew what I would find. On the other hand, Cathy often got up to investigate because she was still concerned. Nevertheless, getting up in the middle of the night only left her more perplexed because she always found our cats sound asleep.

*   *   *

Adam was asleep in his bedroom when he was awoken by the crashing sound of books falling over. He could see a cat on his book shelf; but when he turned on the lights, there was no cat. His bedroom door was shut and our own cats were somewhere else. The phantom cat had materialized just long enough to cause a stir.

The same day that Adam had been startled by the phantom cat, Cathy and the boys decided to go for a drive in the country, where they spotted a black cat running along the side of the road. The cat seemed to be staying just ahead of the car, when it suddenly darted in front of them and disappeared in the brush on the other side of the road.

That wasn't the end of the story either. They drove about ten miles further, until they spotted a church which was where they wanted to turn. There was a black cat running just ahead of them the same as before. Sure enough, our furry feline friend crossed Cathy's path for the second time and completely disappeared in the brush on the other side of the road.

Cathy had a strong feeling that it was the same phantom cat which has haunted our home for many years. After Cathy had finished her story, she got very cold. There's no better indicator of the truth, than a cold vibration.

\*    \*    \*

We had covered our new furniture with silver space blankets to keep the cats at bay. The blankets were flexible and sounded like tin foil, so that we would be alerted, if any of our cats tried to navigate the furniture. While we were watching a movie late at night, I could both hear and see one of the space blankets moving. In fact, I saw two distinct movements under a blanket which was covering the arm of an easy chair. Adam saw both of the movements as well; plus, he saw a cat like our female black cat walk in front of the chair just before the movements occurred. It was a bit dark in the room and I was sitting six feet from the easy chair, but I certainly didn't see any cat.

Adam took the challenge. He rushed over to the arm chair and pressed down on the silver blanket. I was concerned because our small female cat had hidden under the blankets a few times in the past. Nevertheless, my fears were unfounded. There was no cat. I kept staring at the chair until our female black cat suddenly darted out from the other side of the room. She had been sitting beside Adam all along.

# Our ghostly doubles

It was the beginning of the summer of 2007. I had stepped into the washroom and I saw Cathy's hair stand on end when she noted that my shadowy self was still standing beside her. The Germans refer to this phenomenon as a *doppelganger*. They consider a double to be like an evil twin, or a sinister form of bi-location.

In our first haunted home, I would be downstairs in my office and I would be spotted in another place. I was also spotted in two places from the backyard on a least two separate occasions. I can truly say that none of this really caused me any misfortune.

There is another form of ghostly double which precedes a living person and is seen performing their actions in advance. *Vardogr* is an old Norse word meaning a forewarning. When you hear the person walking around, opening doors and even talking before they arrive; then you have a Vardogr. In other words, a Vardogr is a spirit which follows people around and projects their coming. It is a protective spirit and a promise of things to come.

I use to work four nights a week when I was living in my previous home. Every night, my Vardogr would arrive home almost exactly ten minutes before me. It would open doors, walk around and even shout out that it was home. Cathy and Adam were afraid to answer because they knew it wasn't me. They always waited for at least ten minutes until the real me would show up. They knew it was the "real me" because I would do everything exactly like the Vardogr. I would even repeat the same lines.

Adam experienced a double Vardogr one time when both Cathy and I went out for a walk. Adam heard the door bell ring. He looked down and saw "us." He looked back down again and was completely perplexed to find that no one was there. Ten minutes later, we showed up and rang the door bell. We had left our keys at home and we needed Adam to open the door, so we could get in. The double Vardogr had warned Adam in advance.

\*   \*   \*

Spirit mimics and parasites have probably deceived millions of humans throughout the ages. Brad Steiger in his book: "Real Ghosts, Restless Spirits and Haunted Places," goes on record to suggest that spirit masqueraders have never been human. Even though the following sighting defies a logical explanation and emphasizes the futility of trying to fit every paranormal experience into a descriptive category, I do have an interpretation of this event.

Previously, the vardogrs and doppelgangers which we've encountered were identical to the person that they were masquerading. In this case, something was different.

During the summer of 2008, Cathy was doing the washing when she saw a carbon copy of me at the top of the basement staircase. I was at least six years younger than my current self and I was smartly dressed in a brown shirt and beige trousers which I wore when I was a bit thinner.

Cathy called out from the laundry room because she thought it was me. The ghost just disappeared.

In terms of an interpretation of the event, our current home was four years old; so there would be no connection between our previous home and our current home. The real mystery is related to the different time frame. Apparently, spirits can appear as living people from the past. Moreover, spirits don't necessarily appear the way that they are expected to appear either. Consequentially, Cathy identified the time in which my double actually lived and had a fright because she didn't expect the spirit to look any different from the person working downstairs on their manuscript.

# Part Two

## A Selected Journal of the Paranormal

*Jacob was dumped out an easy chair and pushed forward; DVD cases opened by themselves; then the discs were thrown at the people in the room; pictures were tossed about (with the picture becoming separated from the frame); and a screen saver picture of Major General Harrison (Tecumseh's arch enemy) was placed on my computer screen to annoy me; and this was only the beginning.*

# Paranormal events at home and elsewhere (June 14, 2007 – November 4, 2008)

I can only say what I know to be true from what I've experienced. I don't believe that most people what to hear about the evil side of the spirit world. Granted, in the spirit world, it is easier to separate the good from the bad. That may even qualify for paradise. Let's just say that if the world is not a perfect place; then the spirit world might be a bit different from what you might expect.

Fighting ghosts is ultimately a never ending battle. You can have a million notches on your tomahawk and there will always be spirits ready to seek combat with you. Consistent undermining of their efforts works best.

Being "haunted" doesn't make you a victim either. I rejected that label from the beginning and fought back instead. That's why I'm extremely vigilant. In the past, some evil spirits have actually labeled me as the "aggressive one." If that's my reputation, then so be it.

Those who are devoutly pious are just as likely to become victims of cruel and unnatural spiritual attacks as anyone else. Often people think that it is their fault, if these supernatural forces gang up on them. Let me tell you straight up: that is totally *false*. Someone who has the backbone to stand up against harassment is a better target for a higher level spirit and is considered to be more of a challenge. The average person who is typically materialistic is simply too oblivious of the supernatural world to fathom what is really happening.

This is a word of warning. If you intend to "save human souls," you might be considered a "threat to demons;" since your work will likely draw you into direct confrontations with them. Nevertheless, you can always count on the support of the Creator. Just remember that demons often focus on the weaknesses of those who try to interfere with their victims.

The good news is that evil entities usually underestimate their opposition. These evil beings challenged me because they wanted their revenge and that is a poor excuse. End result? They allowed me the opportunity to expose them and their vulnerabilities. I've also passed on two volumes of accounts to you concerning their hostilities (this account and Ghostly Allies); plus, I now have my own war chest.

After writing these words, I woke up to the new day with the words "hello busty." These words were clearly spoken to me in my conscious state. At least some of my spirit visitors have a sense of humour.

\*   \*   \*

*In regards to my challenges along the path of shadows, I believe that the Creator works through us and other spirits, to maintain balance in the universe, through the use of various healing methods such as positive thoughts, actions and words.*

*Also note that power rods are considered to be healing rods and vice versa. Power rods can retrieve, store and magnify white light. Therefore, power rods are an excellent choice, if you need to defend yourself from intruding entities.*

June 14, 2007

Cathy came home from shopping and she was complaining that she was running into everything. I thought she was just dizzy. About ten minutes later, Cathy was in a great deal of pain because of an injured foot. She had hurt her foot because she had been pushed into the furniture. Adam said that I should eliminate the spirits who were pushing her around.

June 15, 2007

Cathy and I both heard footsteps upstairs in the master bedroom while we were downstairs in the family room. I went upstairs to investigate. There was no human or animal anywhere in sight. I retrieved both the peace pipe tomahawk and the crystal power rod and sat across from Cathy. I pointed both of the protective healing weapons upwards. Cathy said that her wrists were tingling and her hands were being buoyed upwards by an energy force. At first, I thought it was our ghostly allies who were paying us a visit, until Cathy asked me to stop. I was bringing in too much energy. She was becoming very light and could feel herself leaving her body. However, she didn't like the sensation. With evil spirits, you can count on retaliation. Within five minutes Cathy felt bad again and I had to whirl the crystal rod around the room.

Shortly afterwards, I wrote Cathy a check. She put the check into her purse and left with Adam to go shopping. Just before she got to her destination, she noted that her handbag was not as bulky. Not only did she find out that her wallet had been taken, she could see exactly where it was in her mind. It had been taken from her bag by inter-dimensional displacement and dumped near a window sill upstairs. She came all the way back home and told Adam exactly where to find it.

A little bit later, our cat was seen flying through the air like he had been kicked. I got the power rod. Before I could do anything, Cathy was punched in the breastbone which is also known as the 3rd chakra. Being punched in the 3rd chakra along with the accompanying "psychic headaches" was part of what Cathy had to endure, on an ongoing basis during the summer of 2007.

July 2, 2007

Jacob had decided to help me feed the cats. He put the food bowls in the middle of the room. I thought that they should be moved. I bent down to move them and the kitchen broom was pushed at me from behind. It hit me. Later on, an item was thrown at Cathy, after she opened the cupboard up to retrieve something. I went upstairs with the power rod and my small finger was cut with something very fine. Both Adam and Cathy had their fingers cut as well. However, Jacob got the worse of it when his eye was cut. It wasn't serious; but it bothered him for the entire evening. Meanwhile Cathy had things thrown at her at least four times during the day. The spirit war continues.

July 15, 2007

Cathy opened the door below the sink and the garbage was pushed out at her and ended up all over the floor.

Later on, she took the boys out for a ride. She was on her way home when a large pick-up truck came up behind her with its bright lights on. She tried to focus on the road ahead, as the truck's headlights burned into her rear view mirror. At the same time, she was surprised to find that she was driving into a blanket of fog about the height of the car. That's when she realized that the fog was right at the same place as the missing farm house.

As soon as Cathy hit the fog, the truck's headlights disappeared. No one saw the truck turn into the place where there should have been a driveway and an old farm house.

The old farm house had been seen by Adam, Jacob and Cathy on the night of a full moon, over a year ago. Cathy described the old farm house as having dark windows on the outside, with a spotlight shining on the outside of the building. She went back to the exact location the next day and found that most of the trees were missing. Moreover, the old farm house was gone. In its place was an old shack.

\* \* \*

Cathy had just being telling me about a light being who looked like a bean pole. The spirit had been watching her work at her desk. She described the ghostly ally as being a white-blue sliver of light, the width of a broom handle. When she looked directly at the spirit, it disappeared. This wasn't the only story she had to tell today.

It was 3:00am in the morning when Cathy started to tell me a story about the local animal hide factory which had been pulled down recently. The land was slanted for redevelopment, but the government had decided that it should be used for green space instead.

There were some old homes in the area in which the management of the hide factory used to live in, according to Cathy. Cathy said that all of the vacant factory land that was for sale was "not good property."

Cathy said that when you visited the area by going around a road loop by the new homes, you were fine. But if you went the other way, by the old homes, you got a horrible feeling of anger and sadness. Adam refused to go back to the area again.

Cathy said that when they tore the factory down, the ghosts who use to manage the factory had nowhere to go. In other words, the ghosts still felt they had the responsibility to look after things there. Now they were being denied. They still haunt the area and they are both sad and angry.

The story of the animal hide factory seemed to twig Cathy's memory and she launched into another ghost story. Cathy claimed a spirit had been exercising on the top floor of our house at night. Almost on cue, we both heard the pounding of feet on the second floor. Since Cathy and I were both standing at the top of the stairs on the second floor, the sound seemed to be coming from Adam's bedroom. However Adam was standing right beside me. As soon as the pounding feet started, Cathy began to feel very cold. I had to ask for the white light to fill our house twice, in order to stop the pounding feet.

July 23, 2007

Both Adam and Cathy mentioned they had heard a sound like "fallen furniture" upstairs, a few times over the past few weeks. The sound of things falling over usually indicates an "escalation in problems." However, I wasn't going to allow that to happen. I started to do my daily five minute patrol, at different times each day. In fact, I got one of them on the stairs today because of the change in schedule.

August 4, 2007

We were just about ready for supper. Both Cathy and Adam felt a very strong chill. I went for the power rod. But I missed my target. About five minutes later, I was thoroughly disgusted when the same spirit stood in front of me and gave off the most atrocious smell.

I didn't say anything. I just got up from my chair and bolted downstairs. I returned with my tomahawk.

Everyone could tell I was very annoyed, when I swung the tomahawk at it. I had no further problems that day.

August 16, 2007

There was a bit of a tiff over Jacob getting to an event on time. It created enough negative energy that a spirit was able to move a chair and push it over on Cathy's foot. Cathy had to sit on the floor with a bag of frozen vegetables on her foot, to help prevent any swelling.

August 18, 2007

On the way home from Fort George we stopped at a fast food place. Jacob was eating some fries. I saw him drop some fries, but no fries fell on the floor. He also seemed totally perplexed that the fries had disappeared. Then he claimed that all of the fries in the bottom of his container had also disappeared. He seemed very concerned that this had happened, so I thought there might be something to it. But I had a long drive home and I was getting tired of the ghostly harassment, so I decided to go back to the car and wait for the others to return.

The parking lot was vacant, except for the person sitting in the car parked next to me. If anyone looked like a dead man, he did. He never moved an inch while I waited.

When Cathy, Adam and Jacob returned, I glanced at the other vehicle. I was shocked to see that there was no one in it. I didn't hear or see him leave either. I asked Adam, if he had noticed anyone in the front seat of the vehicle parked beside us. It spooked him because he *also* thought that somebody had been sitting there. Both Cathy and Jacob thought they saw a movement in the car as we pulled out. It's possible that someone was playing hide and seek; but I doubt it.

I went on the warpath when I got home to make sure everything was under control, but I got a surprise in the morning regardless. Ten black fingerprints were left on the wall in the kitchen. The prints were about adult height and they looked extremely odd.

August 20, 2007

The boys discovered a metallic streak of substance and it was stuck to the upstairs rug. It also looked like something had been dragged across the rug, but there was no possible explanation for it.

Later on, I made some popcorn for the boys. Both Jacob and Adam jumped when a bag of popcorn was taken out of Adam's hand and deposited in the middle of the living room floor. Adam said it was as if a strong breeze had blown the bag away. Both boys agreed that the bag was lifted up and dropped in the middle of the floor.

August 27, 2007

Cathy was reciting another story about a giant hawk which swooped down at her car the other day. Both of the boys were in the car at the time. She stated that the wing span was as wide as the car. She knew that hawks didn't get that large; but they had been following her around for years, so she was use to it by now.

Later on, I was concerned that we needed to leave for Fort Erie right away or we wouldn't have enough time for a visit. Just ten minutes before we were to leave, several things happened.

Jacob saw his bedroom blinds being torn from the wall, snapped in two and thrown on the floor by invisible hands.

At the same time, Cathy came out of the shower. Her clothes had been left on the bed. Now they were missing. I went around the house with my two power rods. I was a bit concerned because I knew that this spirit was very powerful.

No sooner had I left the second floor when I got another call to go to Jacob's bedroom again. He had walked into the bedroom and a spirit had played a chord on his guitar. He described it as an evil chord which was very sharp. I asked for the light a few times to rid the house of the demons from Hell. I asked for the power twice because I wanted to make sure.

The demon was deliberately doing this to mess up my trip. It was a class act on the demon's part to let me know that Hell was on my wave length and ready to rumble when I least expected it. For a normal person, it would have been a terrifying experience.

After our day trip to Fort Erie, I examined the damages which were caused by the demon. I made a speech like a preacher, according to Cathy. She thought I should go on television and convert all the sinners in the world. Instead I kept Jacob up half of the night. The poor ten year old, was still scared out of his wits because of the attack in his bedroom. I explained to him that it doesn't do any good to worry about anything from Hell.

August 29, 2007

I wanted to leave for Fort Niagara by 12:30pm or 1:00pm at the latest. I was shouting to everyone upstairs that we were leaving at 1:00pm since it looked like things were on the late side. I was getting angry because no one except Jacob was ready. Jacob heard me say 1:00pm. Both Cathy and Adam heard 1:30pm. I yelled up several times and I asked them to describe how the sound was coming out. Adam said it sounded slightly muffled, but it sounded like 1:30pm. However, once Adam got to the top of the staircase, he could clearly hear what I really said. Cathy tried it too. She said it was a trick. We were late anyway, but the spirit had his fun.

We stopped off at a fast food place on the way home after our visit to Fort Niagara and I asked Jacob about the trouble in his bedroom the other night. Jacob agreed with me that the ghosts had been more active in trying to prevent us from leaving our home on time. He was about to say something else when he was punched hard in the stomach. He was in a great deal of pain. He felt like someone was turning their fist in his gut. I already had the jet out and I shot the demon with it. Jacob said that the pain left him as soon as I used the jet.

August 31, 2007

I was talking to Cathy about my manuscript while she was preparing breakfast for the boys. The toast came up and she turned around to get the margarine. She practically jumped when she realized that the margarine had disappeared. I had used the tub about ten minutes before. We couldn't find the margarine anywhere. It had disappeared from our dimension.

The second incident of the day occurred outside. Cathy claimed that she had reached down to pick something up from our driveway when she was knocked forward. I saw her go. She looked like she had been kicked by a horse. She couldn't remember anything, but she thought that she might have hit the side mirror on her car. However the mirror was plastic and probably wouldn't have caught her in the forehead. Moreover, she wasn't that close to the car.

At the time I also felt that it was the mirror; however, later on, Jacob was making lemonade. I watched Jacob pour a glass three quarters full for Adam. Within five minutes Adam's glass was full to the brim and there was lemonade all over the counter top. Adam's journal book had been left on the counter and it was soaked in lemonade too. No one had been near the counter either.

Adam agreed with me that we were experiencing more problems than usual. He told me that a pop can had been thrown at him in his bedroom and his guitar had been knocked down.

Another incident occurred, as I was preparing a late night snack. I could smell an evil entity right beside me. I dropped both the knife and the cheese, as I made my way to the basement. I had chosen to ignore the problems throughout the day. Now I was ready to take them on. I retrieved both of my power rods and I requested that all the demon intruders from Hell be banished from our home. I asked for it twice.

Just before bedtime, we checked the fridge for the return of the margarine. The margarine was not there.

September 1, 2007

The margarine had been returned to the fridge by the morning. Things are returned when you ask for them. But sometimes it takes a little longer.

Cathy was asking where Tommy was. Our male black cat was at the bottom of the stairs in the basement. He was looking rather concerned. Cathy said that she heard a cat similar to Tommy a moment before, right beside her. Our phantom cat had made another appearance.

Cathy and I headed off to Toronto while the two boys had a visit with their grandparents in Brampton. While we were in Toronto, we walked by a mammoth dig on Bay Street. Cathy refused to look at the site because it had unleashed things that she didn't want to know about.

She had many connections with different psychics many years ago and one of them told her that there were many parts of Toronto which were particularly bad in the downtown area. The Bay Street development was one of the areas which should not have been disturbed. From my perspective, it looked about five stories deep in the ground like there were on their way to Hell. Perhaps they were.

Cathy mentioned a few places on the way home which she also found frightening. She never imagined that some places could be so off putting at night time, but okay during the daytime. After Cathy made her statement, the electric window on Adam's side opened by itself and I flew into action with my jet in one hand and the steering wheel in the other much to Cathy's amazement.

September 04, 2007

Like a moth to the flame, Cathy couldn't resist going back to a particular bad place. In fact, she took the boys with her. When I asked her why she did it, she said that it was not that bad during the day. There was only one problem. She got more than she bargained for.

A white car pulled out behind her in the haunted area and followed her for miles along side roads, back roads and main roads. The wind shield of the pursuing vehicle was heavily tinted; but Adam said that he could tell that the driver of the haunted car was a woman with long hair.

Cathy signaled left and right and was going nowhere in particular; but this car kept exactly a car's length behind her. Finally, Cathy decided to do a quick turn without any warning and it seemed impossible that the car would be able to make the turn. The white car did indeed speed up and continue on. Nevertheless, it had been following her for a very long time in an area which she normally avoided at night time.

September 7, 2007

Cathy was relatively calm while she was telling me something about being pushed down the stairs while she was carrying a laundry basket, about half an hour before. After she mentioned the incident, she began to complain about a headache and a strong chill. Then she started to feel aggressive and uneasy at the same time.

After I asked for the light, she said that things had improved; but the situation had not been resolved. So I concentrated my will on her with the two power rods. My thoughts were set to eliminate whoever or whatever was causing problems in the house. Whatever it was, it left. Cathy and I both felt it was my job to eliminate the negative powers this time.

I reported that my gunfighter re-enactor coat had been taken away from me in the Ghostly Allies book. It was returned to me today. The coat was needed for a Halloween event that I wasn't aware of at the time. The universe always knows best.

On another note, my brother-in-law told us that his father and uncle were communicating with him. They were both dressed in nice suits and letting him know that they were both promoted to spirit guides. Spirit guides help deceased people go through the transition from our world to the after life.

September 16, 2007

I needed a map of Fort York, so I asked Adam to get it from a book. I saw Adam open the book and the pamphlet was there for one second and then it was gone. Someone was having a game with us.

September 25, 2007

This ghost story actually frightened Adam. Adam and Jacob were outside fooling around in the dark. They were chasing each other, until Jacob decided to go into the house. Adam did a double take when he saw "Jacob" go running around the house again. He chased after him; but he couldn't find him; so he stood on the driveway and waited for Jacob to appear. Instead he saw three people walking down the street towards him. He had a very eerie sense that he knew them well; but he was also frightened of them. They were on the street in plain view, but they seemed to vanish. Adam ran towards them and looked at every avenue of escape; but there was no means of evading him. Adam was walking back towards our house when Jacob appeared. Adam asked him where he had been. He replied that he had been in the house for almost ten minutes and that he had not been running around the house as Adam claimed.

Later on, Cathy told me another story. As I listened, the room became very cold. There was a ghost beside her. She asked for the power rod which I was holding; but I strongly felt that the spirit was of light. She ended up with a headache from the spirit who was trying to communicate with her; but that was it. Meanwhile, I went around the house and did my usual duties with the power rod. By the time I got back, the spirit had left.

September 30, 2007

The sun had gone down and it was one of those Halloween type nights with the fog and mist. Cathy decided that she was not going to give into her fears. So she decided to go to the most haunted place she could think of which was reasonably close to home. Oddly enough, it was foggy everywhere, except for this place. Nothing happened until she got home. I was cooking a turkey in the oven and the kitchen was very warm and stuffy. Jacob was making comments about his plastic arrow which had disappeared from the barrel of his rifle right in front of his eyes.

Then the smell of this pleasant perfume came out of nowhere. Cathy was in the kitchen at the time. She began to complain about a headache, being dizzy and being ice cold at the same time. I walked over and stood right beside her. I was also standing right in front of a hot gas oven. She said it was right behind her. I reached behind her and sure enough my hand went cold. I mean it was really cold. In fact, it stayed cold. I walked out of the kitchen and sat in the family room. I rested my hand on the arm of the chair. My hand was still cold. I asked Cathy if the spirit was still with her. Then I told her that my hand was still cold. She said that the spirit was holding my hand. She strongly felt that the spirit could have been a child. The perfume was only to indicate that she was a good spirit, since evil spirits do not use it based on what I know of them. Within a few minutes the spirit moved back to the kitchen. That's when I decided to go upstairs for a shower.

I was having my shower upstairs, when I started to get a sense that maybe I wasn't alone. I reached out of the shower stall with my left hand to feel the air. I was still warm with the water so I jumped out. I could hear traffic clearly and the room was freezing without any clothes on. I knew right away that my little spirit friend had left the window open for me. I walked over to the window and shut it. I would have known if it was open before I went into the shower on a cold night.

Cathy said that the coldness went away after I went upstairs. Shortly afterwards, the spirit joined us once again in the front room this time. This spirit would have been an interesting one to communicate with. Cathy speculated that it could have been someone from the fort who decided to come home with us. I like to think that it was someone who might have been close to us in another way.

October 5, 2007

We moved some pop cases to the laundry room and placed them on some tall plastic shelving units. Adam went into the laundry room to get a can of pop. He claimed that several cans were thrown at him. Many of the pop cans ruptured and created a mess for Cathy to clean up. I suggested that she bring the rest up to the kitchen. She placed two cases of pop just outside the laundry room. About one minute later I decided to go downstairs to the basement when I noticed a pop can on the first landing. There was also pop all over the basement steps. No one heard anything either. I picked up the can and noticed that the top had been completely ripped off.

October 6, 2007

Cathy, Adam and Jacob were all set to go out for a ride; so that would give me a chance for a much needed rest. I had left the master bedroom door open slightly, so the cats could come and go.

I was in a very restful state when I heard the thumping of a bass guitar. It seemed to be coming from the pillow, so I knew it was in the house. Moreover, I was wondering why Jacob was playing so loud. Actually the bass sounded better than usual. Jacob's amp was very small and it always sounded a bit distorted.

I got up; walked over to the door and peered into the hall way. I could hear the loud bass coming from somewhere upstairs. I only wish I had gone to Jacob's room. Instead I shouted out a few times to Jacob, until I realized that nobody was home. I was annoyed because I knew what it was, but I wanted to rest a little bit more. As soon as I shut the door, the bass stopped suddenly. I rested for another fifteen minutes and there were no further disturbances.

When Cathy returned about three hours later, I began to tell her about the event when she became very dizzy and faint. She said she was being attacked. This time I was ready.

I grabbed both of the power rods from downstairs and I told the spirit that "I had no fear of intruders in my domain and that I had stronger medicine. Moreover, unwanted intruders were not welcomed."

That did it. I got rid of the evil spirit in quick time.

October 12, 2007

I received a copy of "Haunted Britain" in the mail today from Scotland. It was written by Elliot O'Donnell. In my opinion, Elliot O'Donnell lives up to his reputation as one of the greatest ghost hunters of all time. I let Cathy touch the book and she said it felt strange. In the background, the music from the ghost story "A Place of One's Own" was playing. The song also had something to do with Scotland. The bookstore owner had included a note which I also gave to Cathy. She immediately put it down because she felt extremely cold.

I was getting supper about this time and we sat down. Within minutes, the grill from the fireplace was thrown at us. Then a candle and a candle holder which had been placed on a shelf were tossed on to our dining room table. I ran downstairs for the power rod and went around the entire house. Everything was quiet after that.

October 17, 2007

Jacob could smell one of them while he was sitting in an easy chair by Cathy. I did my usual routine with the power rod. Cathy said the negative feeling and the chill were gone. Everything was fine except for one thing. She was practically knocked out by the smell of garlic. Fortunately, the smell of garlic disappeared, after we each had a whiff of it.

After more than five years of major encounters with the supernatural, it was relatively quiet during the fall of 2007.

January 23, 2008

The day I finished my rough draft of *Lessons from the Heavenly Council,* I left it on my desk. Perhaps, the entity intruders in my house considered my accomplishment to be a red flag; so they decided to go through my traps in order to unplug several items from my computer such as the keyboard and the mouse. I believe that some spirits do things for fun, but it's not fun for me, if you have hundreds of them coming after you for all the wrong reasons. One spirit also tried to grab a load of things, but was hit by another trap, as it went up the basement steps with a few trophies. All the things which had being taken materialized and fell down the stairs with an almighty crash. There was a broken serving plate; but that's nothing compared to letting them get away with it.

\*   \*   \*

Cathy asked me to go upstairs with the crystal power rod. She claimed that everything had gone cold in our bedroom. Then Jacob turned on the television. There was no picture. Instead, there was interference. Then the sound turned into a high pitched whine. The volume of the whine increased until it looked like the television was going to explode. This all happened within seconds. Jacob quickly turned the television off.

This was the second time today in which I had to run around the house to keep the lid on things.

February 2, 2008

Cathy had a dream. She was at a party and they were saying, "Oh, look, its Cathy."

Then someone else said that she was not to be there. That's when she ended up back in bed.

The following night she dreamt that she saw a woman with a long 16th century type veil. It was extremely bright behind the woman and Cathy was being told to do something. However, she was also told that she would forget everything which was said. I guess there's no way you can catch that kind of a dream.

February 9, 2008

Cathy got her red amber pendant and her gold jade pendant tangled around her neck, so she took them off and forgot about putting them back on.

I came home from work and found her sitting on a chair nursing her foot with a frozen bag of vegetables. A spirit had just pushed the upright vacuum machine over while she was unplugging it. The hard plastic handle of the vacuum hit her square on the foot. I went around the house with the crystal power rod right away. She was in terrible pain, but things began to ease as soon as I took action.

February 16, 2008

Adam shouted out for me to come upstairs quickly. An unplugged set of computer speakers were full of static and the energy indicators were glowing green. I had my crystal power rod with me and Jacob said to point it down. Then his leg was kicked and the room became ice cold.

Cathy's office was the smallest and warmest room in the whole of the upstairs; yet at that moment, it was the coldest place in the house. I waved the rod around and the temperature went back to normal. However, I was concerned that everything had returned to normal in slow motion.

After we went downstairs together, I had a feeling that it wasn't over; but I wasn't expecting such an intense attack. Cathy was punched between her eyes in the third chakra, one of the favourite human spots for evil spirits to attack. Moreover, she was pushed forward. Meanwhile, Adam was on the couch suffering from a psychic headache.

Jacob gave Cathy a crystal healing rod and told her to put it on her forehead. I gave Adam a crystal rod and told him to do the same. In an emergency, placing a healing crystal rod near your forehead will reduce the negative energy in your sixth chakra.

Jacob had a headache too, but he was not as vulnerable. He grabbed his two power rods from a main floor cabinet. Meanwhile, I ran downstairs to the basement for my tomahawk. Before I did, I ask for the white light. When I returned with the tomahawk, there was a big difference in the ambience around our home. Jacob said that I practically did it myself with the tomahawk. We figured there had been a lot of spirits in on this attack. Personally, I think they are still upset with my writing.

February 22, 2008

This episode re-emphasizes the power of the symbol which becomes part of your belief system over time.

Cathy began to complain about a severe headache just after the boys had returned from school. Both Adam and Jacob replied that they also felt poorly. I could tell from looking at Cathy that something was wrong. She said that she felt like crying and that the atmosphere in our home was extremely negative.

I asked for the white light and for protection. Then I went around the house with the power rod and the tomahawk. Adam felt better, but Cathy felt that something was still not right. I asked for the white light again and that all intruders and unwanted entities should be removed from our home. I positioned my tomahawk in a vertical position with the end of the handle touching the floor. Then I turned the blade completely around three times and asked for protection for the whole house and everyone in it.

Even with the force field around the house, Cathy said that she was still uneasy like someone had walked across her grave. I though I had trapped an entity inside our home because the room was still cold. Then I discovered that the spirit was right beside her. However, I knew that the spirit was a friendly one because I had the power rod pointed right at it.

I decided to check out the effectiveness of my power rod just in case. I pointed the crystal rod towards Cathy and it caused static on the back of her neck from ten feet back. She also said that she felt very strange when the crystal rod was pointed directly at her.

Next, I tried the tomahawk. Cathy could not believe that the tomahawk could be so powerful. She also claimed that the tomahawk was much stronger than the crystal rod.

I decided to retreat and put the power rods away. By the time I had returned, the spirit had left and everything was as it was before. On hindsight, I believe that the tomahawk has become more powerful with my intentions over time.

March 4, 2008

Cathy and Adam were trying to take pictures of Adam's science project in the kitchen. Cathy was frustrated because the digital camera would not work and she had to keep changing the batteries. At the time, she didn't realize that something had prevented her from taking the pictures.

Finally, she noticed that a solid plastic container of solution was leaking everywhere on the table. She also noticed that the plastic container was completely cracked because it had been squeezed. That's when she called for the power rod.

The next day Cathy began to get the shakes after viewing a photograph that was taken just before I arrived with the tomahawk. It was the best photo of a shadow entity that I've ever seen, thanks to the cat and mouse game that she had to play with the camera. In the photograph, there was a human sized, shadow like figure which looked like a black knight. There appeared to be two eyes peering out from a hood like face. We could clearly see a hand on the counter table which looked like it was going to grab the glass. Moreover, Adam said that the seven foot figure he saw upstairs several weeks ago looked similar. There were a few more sightings of shadow entities around our house afterwards. That's when I decided to do something about it in dreamtime.

March 26, 2008

I was in some drab grey areas of the astral plane during dreamtime, until around 4:30am. That's when my spirit was pulled back to my body for a good reason.

There was a shadow entity hovering over me, just below my chest. My sense of awareness was similar to the time when I was attacked by several demons and I was unable to move. In this case, the tingly sensation in my mind meant that I wasn't totally back in my body; nevertheless, I was fully conscious of what was happening. I also knew that the spirit was similar to the shadow entity which I had seen in a picture that Cathy had taken in our kitchen about three weeks before. Still I couldn't make out what this entity looked like.

I didn't want to move because I had a firm hold on the entity with both hands; but I couldn't hold my grip outside of my body for more than ten seconds. That's when the tingly, mind-felt sensation stopped and I was fully returned to my body. Because I was no longer in my spirit form, the entity was allowed to escape.

So what is the role of your aura in all of this? The outer shell of your aura is like a force field which activates a sensory alarm and initiates a response. In other words, your aura acts like a tracking system that can detect invisible beings when they are within your personal space. Just make sure that you ask for the white light to fortify your aura on the occasions when you think you might need extra protection.

March 31, 2008

Anyone who has faced the spirit world on a regular basis has had a variety of experiences from the horrific to the outright comical. This one is from the latter category.

Today, I came across some imposing ghost tracks. I was thinking about people like Peter Underwood and Harry Price who were both past presidents of the Ghost Club; plus, thousands of other ghost seekers the world over who have used powder for years, to try and track ghosts in haunted places. They would have been interested in my findings.

I was running a bit low on kitty litter this morning, so I decided to add a little plant powder to the usual mix. I was wearing my black polyester track pants at the time because I was getting ready to do my exercises on the gliding machine. About five minutes later, I looked down at my pants and discovered hand prints all over both of my pants legs, both up and down. The hand prints were very large and they were placed in such a way that they would be the opposite of what I could have done. The interesting thing was that there were so many of the prints. Someone had taken advantage of the plant powder to "impress me." Naturally, I didn't feel a thing. Cathy said they were definitely someone else's hands.

April 1, 2008

This incident took place during dreamtime. I was writing at my desk in the spirit world, when a shadow entity came up behind me and threw a cloak over my body. I bit its hand because I sensed that this entity was bad news. The result was transformation. My teeth became more like a wolf and my breath was of fire. I faced the entity and it was over in a moment. Then I was back in my conscious state.

This vision also had symbolic implications. The entity who tried to cover me with a cloak was trying to shield itself from my writing, by keeping me in the darkness. However, I believe that even in total darkness, there can be light.

When I was nineteen, I went overseas to visit England. While I was staying at the Ambleside youth hostel on Lake Windermere in the English Lake District, another traveler at the hostel was startled by a long audible speech that he heard from me as I was sleeping. He thought it was quite bizarre and he was frightened by it. At the end of the speech, he heard me say: "In total darkness, can there be light?"

My answer to that question is this: For those who are open to the truth, there is always light.

April 10, 2008

The one thing that I've learned is when there is something evil in the house, it will either return to the scene of the crime or it will reappear after you begin to talk about it. I retrieved both of my power rods and I said that if it was not of the light, then it was not welcomed because I was of the light of God. Now I could find out just how evil it really was.

It had lost some of its power from my words, but it had not left. I came to the conclusion that it really was evil. I went around the house with the healing rods and asked for the white light. Then I directed that all negative energy should be released from our home. Everything was normal after that. There's nothing better than a good spring cleaning.

April 19, 2008

I've learned to appreciate the significance of Passover, after we began practicing the ceremonies a few years ago, according to Cathy's upbringing,

Cathy and I were returning from Toronto. She had bought some wine for the Passover ceremony. Because she was carrying a bottle of wine around with her, she began to look at carrying bags which were on sale. She never said anything to me about buying the wine, since I don't drink alcohol; or why she wanted the carrying bag. Because I was preoccupied with a book that I was reading, I wasn't even aware that she was carrying a wine bottle.

She found a carrying bag on sale, but she didn't buy it because there was no price listed on the sale tag. Because I was somewhat lukewarm towards the purchase, she decided to leave it behind in the store.

We were about half way back to the parking lot, when I saw Cathy's foot come up and actually kick the same carrying bag, after it materialized out of nowhere, on a busy street in downtown Toronto. The amazing thing about this incident was not the unexpected appearance of the carrying bag; rather it was her conscious mind requesting the bag at the time that the carrying bag materialized because she was afraid that the wine bottle might drop and break. The universe agreed with her and provided the means to transport the wine back to the car.

Many people are under the illusion that their thoughts and actions don't matter, if no one is paying attention. If anything, the universe is waiting to hear from you. There is no reason to hide from the truth.

April 23, 2008

I retrieved the power rod and I whirled it around Cathy's 3rd chakra area after she complained about a chest pain. Then I stated that any spirit who was intruding should go to the light. I repeated the whirling crystal rod technique around her 3rd chakra area and pointed the crystal rod towards the heavens. Then I repeated my demand that the spirit intruder should go to the light. The spirit was exorcised immediately because of the healing rod and my second demand.

Whirling the crystal rod in a clockwise direction, using 360 degree circles draws the spirit out. Whenever, Cathy has a chill and I haven't been able to locate the spirit, I usually wait for her to feel the chill again. Then I whirl the crystal rod around her and draw the spirit to me. To target the spirit, I stop the whirling and point the crystal rod, or I sweep the space in front of me, along an imaginary horizontal line with my peace pipe tomahawk. If the spirit has been particularly difficult, a swift horizontal line cut with the tomahawk is the preferred method.

Later that night, I was a bit careless. Cathy and Adam were sitting in the upstairs office and I was in the middle of my rounds. I stopped to talk to them about something. That's when Cathy began to complain about a sharp pain in her arm. I realized right away that I was pointing the crystal power rod at the exact spot. So I turned the concentrated power away from her arm and everything was fine. I told them that the only reason I was still writing about spirits and ghosts was because of the universal light force. The light force is so unbelievably potent; yet, so few people are aware of its potential.

Here are a few reminders. Your purity of intent to protect others is all that is necessary, if you want to utilize the universal light force. In some cases, your purity of intent can be compromised by a negative outbreak or negative behaviour. If your purity of intent has been compromised, it's better to wait five minutes and then start again like nothing happened.

Also, be aware that evil spirits may attack the light or change direction. Either way they are defeated.

Finally, when you are exorcising powerful spirits with a crystal power rod, you need to be aware of the voids that you create. Powerful spirits are attracted to the void like a moth to the flame. The typical time it takes from being exorcized, until it's time to take out their revenge is approximately five minutes. Nevertheless, during the post-void phase the full power of the universal light force will still be available to you. In most cases, you will be finished after you exorcize the vengeful spirits on your second attempt.

Here is a statistical breakdown. Over 90% of intruders are exorcised on the first attempt. More powerful spirits and most groups of spirits usually require a double dose. However, a powerful multitude of spirits or a strong energy force may require as many as six or more attempts. Fortunately the last category is rare; but I've had more than my share.

April 25, 2008

Adam tried to joke about it; but he felt very uncomfortable about saying it. He said that he swore that he saw Satan. I only wish that I could have been there.

Cathy and the boys had gone for a drive in the country. They were going down a side road in a rural area when someone just came out of the ditch.

The first thing they noticed was that this person did not look like a farmer. He was entirely dressed in black. His greasy looking slicked back hair was shoulder length. He also had a well trimmed goatee.

The most striking feature of this person was his stare. He looked at Adam with the most grim and evil looks that Adam had ever experienced in his life. Cathy was too overcome with this individual's look of hatred to even look at him. She claimed that the horror and foreboding wouldn't leave her until she turned onto another road. Then everything went back to normal.

I asked Adam if the evil looking man in black had disappeared after they drove by him. Adam said he was too scared to turn around and look again. Once was enough.

May 27, 2008

Cathy had been knocked over on her back. One minute she was standing, the next she was flat out. She also had a terrific headache that wouldn't stop, until I removed the problem. Unfortunately, it's these random, aggressive acts by spirits which make me continually vigilant.

It only takes one bad turn to break your neck and who would ever suspect anything other than your own clumsiness. The solution is to increase your awareness of the spirit world and keep your protective strategies close at hand.

When someone has a bad turn for no explainable reason, I usually sweep the house with the power rods. But this time, I was a bit annoyed because Cathy could have been hurt. I stated that the unwanted intruders should return to the lake of fire where they belong. I also visualized a lake of fire. I was a bit more dramatic than usual and it wasn't my intention to blurt out the religious jargon in a priest like fashion. However, sometimes I can't honestly understand how some of them got out of the fire pit in the first place.

July 30, 2008

The boys had arrived home after being out of the house for the day. Even though it was getting dark, it was still very warm outside, so they were looking forward to a dip in the swimming pool in our backyard. Normally, they stayed out in the pool for an hour; but today they were back inside the house within five minutes. They were both complaining that there was something wrong with the pool. Jacob claimed that he smelled like manure and that the water in the pool was like sewage. Adam said they same thing as they both ran for the shower. Jacob told me later that he scrubbed and scrubbed with soap to get rid of the smell.

I had to go out and cover the pool myself. The first thing I did was scoop some water in order to examine it. Then I splashed my face with it. I even put my arm into the pool and reached down to the bottom. The water was perfectly normal. However, I could smell manure in the air. We lived in the country and it was a humid day, so the manure smell must have come from a local farmer's field.

I told the boys that it was a trick. Adam had worn his shirt in the pool because of the mosquitoes. He claimed that his trunks and his shirt both smelled like sewage; but when he examined his swimming clothes after I told him the truth, there were no offensive odours present. Jacob couldn't believe what he was hearing. He swore that he had an awful stench all over him, even while he was upstairs showering. Now Jacob had to admit that his bathing clothes were also perfectly fine.

It was one of the best tricks that the spirits had ever played on us.

August 13, 2008

The filter hose to the swimming pool had been tampered with and the water from the pool had drained out overnight. If this had been someone else's pool, it would have been vandalism. As I was talking with Cathy about it, a toy soldier from behind her on the shelf was thrown at her.

I went around the house a few times with the power rods; but the spirit evaded me. In the meantime, Cathy had her cosmetic case thrown at her while she was in the upstairs bedroom. While she investigated the problem, she noticed that her transistor radio had been taken apart and the bathroom door had been locked from the inside.

Afterwards, she decided to take the boys out for a drive. On the way back home, everyone felt a sudden chill just before Cathy was punched in the face and given a bloody nose. The impact of the blow wasn't the same as a human blow; but the result was the same. Let me be very clear on this point. Powerful spirits can assault you.

August 14, 2008

Since we leave our cars outside, the car doors are always locked. Just recently, a car door had been left wide open overnight on two separate occasions, for no reason.

After the first time, a concerned neighbour knocked on the door when she noted that Cathy's car door had been left open all morning. We thanked the neighbour and left it at that.

I thought that the aggressive spirit which had assaulted Cathy and left her car door opened on two occasions was the same culprit. The bathroom door in the master bedroom had been locked many times over the past couple of months and I was beginning to put things together. This intruder had been lying low in order to gain enough power to attack. The next step would be a showdown with me.

We had been feeding a stray cat on our porch over the past few weeks and I had been putting his tray out in the morning. Today I discovered that he had brought up some of his food. So I brushed the regurgitated food off the porch.

Then I noticed a dead bubble bee. The bee looked a little weird because it was all black with no other colouring. I thought nothing of it, as I swept the dead bee away as well.

We were on our way to Fort George; so I went back into the house and asked everyone to hurry up. At the last minute, Cathy's purse went missing. I asked for it to be returned to its rightful owner and I brought in the white light. We found the purse hidden under a stack of pillows a few moments later. Just after that both the bathroom and the master bedroom doors were slammed shut. There was no one around them and the windows were all closed. One of our cats would have been locked in the master bedroom as a result, so Cathy positioned a chair in the bedroom doorway. That's when the entity threw a box of items at her from a dressing room table.

Cathy came downstairs and told me what happened. I shouted out to the entity that if it didn't leave by the time I got back, it would be someplace better. I was being a bit sarcastic for a change because I didn't want to chase after it.

As I left the house, I noticed bits of food all over the porch again. It was almost like I had not swept the porch less than ten minutes ago. Our hungry cat would not have made a mess either. He always ate every little crumb of food, not matter where it was. I looked a bit closer at the food and I was a bit surprised to find that the food was the same regurgitated food that I had swept over the side of the porch less than ten minutes ago. Not only that, the dead bumble bee was back on the porch. It wasn't a coincidence either because I recognized it. Now I knew I was going to have to make good on my promise to exorcize the unwanted intruder later on.

Because of the physical assault in the car the day before, I also knew that the spirit world would be helping me out more than usual. I was in Niagara-on-the Lake, outside of a shop and waiting for Adam and Cathy to appear. Jacob and I were talking about the items which the Council had asked me to get a few years ago. When Cathy and Adam came out of the shop, they didn't see us because we were standing behind a few tall flowers. Perhaps the spirits wanted us to finish our conversation before we were discovered.

Finally, I though about the judge's wig that the Council had ordered for me. I had received the wig four years ago; but I had never used it. I began to think I had been a fool. I finally asked Jacob if it would work. He thought about it for a minute and then he said that I would find out for myself. He also said that the white soldier's wig which was ordered at the same time was for an assistant.

The Council had told me that I had been a warlock during the middle ages in Britain. I was sentenced to death at some point in time and I came back as a judge who sentenced witches. Because I still have strong connections with my previous incarnates, linking symbols from one incarnate to another boosts one's power. Moreover, it's not just the incarnate; it's the symbolism of the judge's wig and the power that the bearer brings to the symbol which is important.

It was very cold and late when we arrived home. I proceeded to patrol the house. I had my jet around my neck, my two power rods in each hand and my judge's wig on my head. No one had seen me with the wig on before, so they had to get use to it. As they say, it's the results that count.

From a psychic's point of view, instead of cold and nasty, we got a different result. Often it had been less than positive, after returning home from Fort George. This time it really was different. First of all, I could tell that the wig was very special, so I went around the house twice. Adam said that he felt incredibly peaceful. The ambience of our home gave one a feeling of order, stability and balance. The chaos of the negative side had also been removed.

The next morning, I found the dead bumble bee on the porch for the third time. Perhaps, it was a bumble bee curse. Since I didn't have an opportunity to eliminate the spirit before our trip to Fort George, I wasn't surprised or concerned. There was only one thing left to do and that was to bury the dead bumble bee along with the curse.

August 21, 2008

I received a book in the mail today called "Ghost Hunters" by Ed Warren the famous demonologist. When I first examined the book,

I didn't notice anything unusual about it. But after I had put the protective plastic cover over the book wrap, I could detect cigar smoke. I became suspicious, so I reached for the power rod and exorcized any vibrations which were connected with the book. Then I filled the vacuum with my own positive vibrations. That only took about half a minute; but at that exact moment, Adam was screaming at me to come upstairs quickly. All hell had broken loose. Cathy was feeling terrible and several items had been thrown.

Whoever had been associated with the book had caused an energy imbalance in our home. We captured several renegade spirits and sent them off; however, we couldn't get rid of the "exorcized spirit." I asked Cathy to hold the book. Cathy said that there was nothing wrong with the book, but the previous owner didn't want to be separated from it. In fact, the spirit wanted to re-attach itself to my book; so I reinforced my vibrations, by pointing the power rod at the book. Then I told the spirit to go to the light.

The earthbound spirit started to cause more problems with Cathy, so Jacob set up four of his pyramids on the living room floor beside Cathy. I also retrieved my jet dragon and gave it to her. Cathy was now completely protected from the spirit.

Then Jacob put a black pyramid with a Celtic cross on the book. Later on, I placed one of my Native American Indian totems near the book. Cathy confirmed that the previous owner had left us after the brief ceremony. The next morning I put the book in a well protected book case with the totem as insurance.

This is a reminder to anyone who buys used articles. Although I can't say that this happens very often, it only has to happen once to make you into a believer. Make sure that you place protection around your used item; just to make sure that it is really is yours. Otherwise, you may be haunted by an inanimate object.

August 22, 2008

I was doing my rounds just before our evening movie and I was in a hurry. As a result, I missed the laundry room on the main floor. I put the power rods away and went back upstairs. I was cooking some popcorn in the kitchen when Adam asked me if I heard a loud hissing in the front room. He claimed that it sounded just like the hissing of a large serpent. I have often associated these odd sounds with cat haters. However, the cat hater usually sounds like a human. You can create this sound yourself by sucking air through your teeth and drawing back on your bottom lip. However, this time it was not directed at the cats. It was a sign of hatred towards us, according to Adam.

In the meantime, Cathy had walked into the laundry room where the intruder had been hiding previously. She came dashing out saying that it was still in there. I retrieved the power rods one more time and dealt with the problem.

Cathy also said that I should train the power rods on the large white cluster crystal which was located about ten feet from where I exorcized the haunted book the night before. The spirit which came with the Ghost Hunter book had not gone to the light after all. Instead it had become disoriented and was trapped by the closest cluster crystal. Therefore, we had to do the right thing according to Dr. Wickland and release the spirit from the cluster crystal. We directed the spirit to the white light again and this time we were successful.

November 4, 2008

Today was the U.S. presidential election, but I was greeted by a different kind of news. Most paranormal incidents had been very minor around the house because I had boosted our protective household energy shield with some extra crystals in copper bowls. Nevertheless, with the coming of Halloween, I noted that something was amiss. There had been a few difficulties and finally one of our new dining room chairs was broken for no reason.

Jacob had been home for the day after I had made arrangements to have the chair taken back to the furniture store for repairs. He was taking the chair out to the car when a demon grabbed him by the foot. He felt the pressure on his ankle and he fell over.

After I had returned home, a speaker was thrown at Jacob from the top of a cabinet, so I had to take action against the entity. I asked the demon to come to me, as I whirled the crystal rod. I did the pyramid formation; then I crossed the tomahawk with the crystal power rod. In a very authoritarian voice, I stated that the entity was banished from our house for twenty years and that it would be sent far away.

You might ask yourself, "How was this demon able to counter a strong household shield in the first place?"

More powerful demons are able to weaken a protective household shield for a short period of time; however, it costs them a significant amount of power to do so. That's why I was able to dispatch the demon in less than a minute using a true and tried method.

# Part Three

Removing Shadow Entities
from your home using the
ULF Approach

*Energy disturbances not only haunt us; they can make us physically ill and mentally unbalanced. If you want peace and abundance in your life, you need to eliminate the negative energies in your environment and the best way to neutralize negativity is to touch base with the universal light force. This force is also known as the white light. If you use the ULF approach, with a few other necessary items, you'll be set up for action in no time. Fixing most problems should only take about five minutes a day; whereas some exorcists spend hours dealing with similar phenomena. That is not to say that exorcism is not necessary in some cases. If someone has been completely taken over by a demon and is too weak to resist, then that is another matter altogether. Nevertheless, the ULF way of eliminating negative energies has been shown to be extremely effective against both powerful demons and aggressive human energies. It has also been shown to be highly effective in cases of mild possession.*

*The power source of the universal spirit connects us all; therefore, the universal light force or white light as it is known can sometimes be used in unexpected ways, even if one is not fully conscious of its power. This may seem elementary, but the key to strengthening your secret psychic power is done by calling for the universal light force on a constant basis, for the sole purpose of maintaining a light fortress.*

# 3.0 Introduction to the universal light force

Living with psychic influences from humans is a growing concern in our world. Those who do not recognize that they are being manipulated by aggressive psychic energies can themselves become emotionally prone to the energies associated with fear and aggression.

The same thing can be said about uninvited entities once they infiltrate your living space. When the veil is lifted, your household may experience a weird and not so wonderful assortment of paranormal activity that might be increasing difficult to tolerate, depending on your energy and stress levels.

If your first reaction to psychic phenomena is fear, worry or anger, then the intrusive psychic energy is probably unwanted. Fortunately, there is an alternative to reverting to fear and aggression. By eliminating all intrusive negative phenomena within your living space, you will also increase your connection to the superior power of the Universal Light Force. The Universal Light Force, or ULF for short, is the only power that you need to tap into in order to help yourself, to what is rightfully yours.

\*　　\*　　\*

Even though my writing has been responsible for a great deal of personal harassment from hostile entities, the attacks themselves have helped me to improve my defensive tactics. In the beginning, I lacked knowledge of the spirit world and my fears and anger were not in check; so my guardians helped me to get a head start. Then I realized that they would not solve all of my problems. In fact, they seemed to be less involved as

I became more powerful. At some unknown point in time, I decided to put myself on the fast track. However, the so called "fast track" has taken me at least seven years to get this far.

*   *   *

When I first began to work with energy, I found it to be a bit complex. Some symbolic items and crystals were effective against some powers while other protective items appeared to have some limitations. At the time, I thought that most symbols had to be combined to be effective. Then I discovered that most of my "protection" could be compromised by powerful spirits. But it also occurred to me that power rods were special because they always worked to some extent against evil entities. That is why I took the route of becoming more proficient with power rods.

*   *   *

After I obtained my red and gold peace pipe tomahawk, I promptly hung it up on my office wall like a trophy. A few weeks passed and my youngest son Jacob, who was only about six years old at the time, finally said to me: "Dad, I don't know why you don't use the tomahawk. It's at least as powerful as the crystal power rod."

He might have had some coaching from our spirit allies; but his statement proved to be correct many years later. The red and gold tomahawk was indeed the most effective protection that I possessed; however, it would take me several more years before I was capable of building a sustainable light fortress.

Accordingly, the lessons in this book focus on both the light warrior and the building of a light fortress using the UFL approach. Ultimately, the purpose of a light fortress is to keep most entity intruders out of your living space. Those powerful entities that are still able to negotiate your energy fields will be removed on a timely basis with minimal effort, once you have everything in place.

Moreover, you should never forget that you are an energy being, who has some say in *how you want to guide* the universal power.

To begin setting up a long term solution for all your paranormal problems, please go to part four.

For *emergency situations* continue on and read "the quick fix."

# 3.1 The quick fix

As indicated in the previous passage, this book will give you an outline on how to balance energy fields within your living space, over the longer term. Nevertheless, those readers in need of a "quick fix blueprint" have several options available to them.

## Recommended quick fix plan

In order - from the most recommended to least recommended:

### I. Crystals

Crystals lead the way because they amplify and manifest changes. If you are fearful of the unknown, I would recommend you take the following steps.

> ➤ wear a protective jet pendant;
> ➤ obtain a power rod; and
> ➤ place some crystals in a copper bowl at home.

I would also advise you to touch the main crystal in your copper bowl each day, in addition to your power rod and your pendant. Remember when things are tough, consistent handling of your crystals contributes to the ULF. Moreover, always be positive and be at one with the universe when handling crystals.

Some of the crystals that you may wish to place in your copper bowl are as follows:

- agates
- amber
- amethyst
- aquamarine
- black jade
- black obsidian
- black tourmaline
- bogie stone
- carnelian
- flint
- fluorite
- jet
- iron pyrite
- magnetite
- smoky quartz
- tourmaline
- turquoise

Please note that one copper bowl of crystals is sufficient for a household shield; however, it's hard to stop at one. For additional protection, place a copper bowl of crystals on each floor; or in specific problem areas.

# II. Essential oils and incense

Essential oils and incense help to keep problems around the homestead under control. Tree essentials work extremely well.

For example:

- cedarwood
- eucalyptus
- juniper
- pine
- sandalwood

Other recommended essentials are:

- benzoin
- frankincense
- lavender
- peppermint
- sage

I actually burned cedar branches in my home after I ran out of sage one time. I definitely don't recommend that you try that. Instead, try a few drops on a special oil burner or lamp ring.

If you are using incense, remember to place the ashes in a container. If you move, you may cremate all of the collected ashes in a hot fire.

# III. Harmonics

Singing bowls, bells and gongs work; but they are a very short term solution because you will have to keep working with them every half an hour or so. As such, they are really only a level one with level two potential. *(Note: Please refer to the three levels of intervention).* In particular, a few good whacks on a decent sized gong should subdue an entity attack. A rattle which has symbolic qualities (like a drawing of a snake for example) would also have level two potential. Nevertheless, a bugle or a military drum is much more effective, if you are being attacked.

# IV. Feng Shui

Some practices like Feng Shui have been hit and miss with me and that is why I hesitate to recommend them. I've seen elaborate set-ups in other homes which haven't worked either (so much for the ancient arts of breaking up negative energy on a consistent basis). Moreover, I find most of the Feng Shui literature to be highly impractical if you're a messy person. (I hope the authors of such literature have a sense of humour if they read this). Anyway, I'm more concerned about entity attacks then they are; so there you have it.

My advice is to avoid as many poison arrows as you can by deflecting energy where necessary (now I'm serious). But trust me - an elaborate and expensive Japanese garden with running water will not eliminate the shadow people in your basement.

Moreover, my Feng Shui mirrors actually became portals for evil spirits and my Feng Shui bells and whistles didn't amount to much either.

My conclusion is that Feng Shui is not for amateurs and it should not be seen as a comprehensive solution for most paranormal problems. Nevertheless, I'm sure that Feng Shui works in some situations and that is why, I've included it here.

# Levels of intervention

I've broken down the levels of intervention, so that you know how serious you need to be when you are dealing with paranormal problems. All items used at the lower levels can be used with the higher level suggestions as well.

## Level I

Description:

- an uncomfortable feeling that someone is watching you
- you can sense something is wrong, but you can't see, hear or smell anything specific

Solution:

- religious symbols
- candles
- incense (the real McCoy; not the fake stuff)
- music (Gregorian is good)
- essential oils

# Level II

Description:

- This really is the beginning of a paranormal problem.
- You can hear, see or smell odd things such as:
  - ➤ the smell of garbage or bad odours
  - ➤ you see a shadowy figure or an odd light
  - ➤ your pet dog or cat gets upset at something for no reason and this keeps happening
  - ➤ you can hear things falling over, but nothing is amiss
  - ➤ items are thrown, moved or knocked over for no apparent reason
  - ➤ the room temperature changes for no particular reason (need further proof)
  - ➤ items disappear and reappear elsewhere (need further proof)

Room temperature changes can indicate good spirits on occasion, so you'll need further proof of a paranormal problem.

If you notice that items have disappeared and then you find them in a more practical place that is not necessarily a bad thing either. Sometimes good spirits like to help out. Usually it makes sense and it can even be amusing on occasion. Don't worry about it unless things start to disappear without a trace. Also, if you ask for something back and the item returns, then you may also be getting help from the good side.

If things start to move around and disappear on a constant basis and they are not coming back in a timely manner, then there could be a serious problem. Still, I would say that you need further proof (like bad smells, a sense of unease and other negative signs). In other words, don't overlook the fact that you have guardian spirits too.

Solution:

Use along with level I recommendations:

- smudging with sage
- crystal power rod
- jet pendant
- household shield
- Lord's Prayer
- personal symbols and jewelry
- singing bowl
- gongs
- bells
- rattles
- crystals in a copper bowl

If you adopt a religious symbol as a personal symbol, then that particular religious symbol should be considered a level II recommendation.

# Level III

Description:

- The paranormal problem persists or escalates.

Solution:

- If the problem persists or escalates, then you will need two power rods and additional resources.
- But before you start to accumulate more protective items (such as an extra power rod), work on asking for the white light and

ask that all unwanted intruders be removed from your home while you do your patrol.

- Repeat the above procedure five minutes later (for the second time), just to be sure.

- The next step is to study chapter four and begin to think and act like a light warrior.

# Part Four

## The Importance of Personal Symbols in Combating Evil

*Through symbols you can increase your personal powers, in addition to managing your fears when confronting adversity. We weren't given all the answers about what living energies we have to share our planet with and I don't mind saying that I'm glad that I can't see everything around me. I have digital pictures of soldiers from centuries old battles, who have shape shifted to look more like evil aliens or hellish human parodies. If you actually saw these images in real life, I doubt whether you would voluntarily go into the dark places where they dwell.*

*Shape shifting is normal enough; but being attacked by unknown entities from the astral plane (or fourth dimension) is not acceptable. Shadow entities have always been around; but now they're becoming more brazen. Humans have created conditions on the Earth plane which invite shadow entities into every possible situation. Your best plan is protection. Protecting yourself and your family, from hostile entities will alleviate negativity in your living environment and reduce your stress levels significantly.*

# 4.0 How to cope with the unseen world

The Earth plane is a dense place of low vibrations. It's also the best school of hard knocks in the universe. Only the bravest souls want to come here. Since Karma returns negative thought forms in slow motion compared to the higher frequencies, places of lower vibrations take much longer to transform their negativity into positive changes. That is why believing in your strengths is the best anecdote to negativity. Inner strengths attract the best frequencies from a higher dimension and allow you to counter inferior thoughts with positive thoughts. You don't have to be a genius with your words; it's the thought that counts. The solution is in the magic of believing.

# 4.1 An introduction to personal symbols

Symbols provide us with one of the most powerful forms of energy in the universe. Once you have identified your personal symbols, you will have the most powerful form of protection from invading energy possible.

Here's an example of how two powerful symbols can be put together. When I had my problems with demons in my previous home, the Council of Elders and the Archangels placed their seals on the correspondence which was delivered to me. The correspondence was always delivered by my Mastery of Life angel. There was so much power in their respective seals that negative entities could not copy them. The reaction of negative entities to the seals would be similar to vampires being burned by a crucifix.

Nevertheless, some psychic protection remedies are only effective against those who recognize their significance. For example, the Star of David may not be used against a spirit with other religious beliefs, who does not recognize the symbol. That is why the bearer of a symbol must believe in the power of the symbol and its purpose.

Symbols can also be used for negative purposes. The Nazi regime used the swastika and slogans to invoke the occult. However, when you invite negative forces to do your bidding for personal gain; you have to pay the price eventually.

# 4.2 Symbols

Symbols are spiritual reminders which encourage us and guide us throughout our lives. Your response to a symbol is based on your own unique understanding of what the symbol means. You can only use protection which feels right for you. If you believe that it works, then that intention will be transmuted into action.

Whatever symbols you choose to adopt, you will want to fortify your aura by projecting the energy into your energy field. Think of how the symbol is centered over your heart chakra and expand it outwards until it fills your entire aura. After using a symbol for a period of time, you can use its power to fill your entire household.

A talisman can be created by drawing an appropriate symbol on a piece of paper or parchment. You only need to focus your will and your intent as you create it.

Another suggestion is that you seek out your personal totem animal in dreamtime. If a totem animal comes to you in a dream and your entire being resonates with its protective power; then you can use your totem animal as a talisman.

Whatever you choose for a talisman, you need to charge it with your particular aims and desires. You should also keep it close to you or on your body.

Many ready made symbols which are found on talismans are universal because they have been in use for thousands of years. For example, Solomon's seal works well because of the vibrations and associations set up over the ages. Nevertheless, the universal symbols work best when they are charged to your particular vibration and needs. Accordingly, any symbol will be more powerful when the creator of the symbol visualizes the kind of protection which is required. For instance, the creator of a talisman may want to strengthen their aura, so they will choose an appropriate symbol for that particular task.

Wearing a symbol, holding it and even breathing on it will attune it to your vibration and imbue it with further power. A repeated request to the universe for protection will also be necessary when the situation requires it.

One of my symbols is a replica 18th century peace pipe tomahawk. Another one of my symbols is the Atlantean power rod. I always hold the Atlantean power rod in my dominant hand and the tomahawk in the other. My built-up energy is released through the power rods. White light can be requested for additional power.

This is how I would visualize my tomahawk. The tomahawk's single, golden blade is attached to a peace pipe. There are colourful red feathers and blue ribbons with red and blue beads on silver chimes. The wooden handle is wrapped in red suede and wolf hair, and secured with gold buttons. The blade and the feathers are bound to the wooden handle with golden suede leather. Moreover, the tomahawk can be visualized as a means of protection and utilized in dreamtime to keep evil entities away.

In summary, any symbolic tool can help an individual with their sense of awareness and consciousness, along with their physical, mental and spiritual abilities and talents.

# 4.3 The power of symbols

This incident concerns one of the most serious encounters which I've had with demons. I was sleeping on the couch in my previous home when I was awoken by thuds coming downstairs. Whatever it was, it was coming for me.

My plan was to grab the tomahawk which I thought was right beside me, hanging from an exercise bike. I was not conscious of any difficulty until I made a move to get up. I was on my back at the time and I tried to lift my head. At first I thought there was something wrong with me because I couldn't move. But I knew that if I didn't get up soon, then something else might happen. Perhaps that something else did happen.

A powerful force was holding me in check. Even though my head was being held back, the pressure felt more like it was inside my head. Several demons were trying to take me over; but I knew that my mind was much too strong for them. Once I began to resist, I realized that my body was also being held on the couch by their invisible hands. I would have to co-ordinate my mind with my body in order to release myself from their grip. Now, the only thought in my mind was to reach for the tomahawk.

I remember using all of my will power in order to break free. Then I kept up my resistance, until they let go. After I jumped up, my mind was still disoriented from the ordeal. I reached for the tomahawk beside me. However, it wasn't there. I just stood there for about five seconds, until I realized that I had foolishly left the tomahawk in my office that night. It had been a perfect time for them to attack.

My office was adjacent to the den where I was sleeping, so it took me another five seconds to retrieve it and return to the demons. I was able to exorcise them from our home within a few moments of my return. I knew in my mind that the tomahawk had done a complete job of it and I went back to sleep with full confidence in the supreme power of the universe in all matters.

Another incident occurred late one night. Cathy had begun to cry quite violently while she was still asleep in bed. I had to shake her shoulder to get her back from dreamtime. She said that she had been stabbed in the back by something unseen. The pain that she was experiencing was just above the shoulder blades. She could barely control herself as she sobbed very openly. She was also starting to panic because she felt that the problem was due to an entity.

The first strategy I tried was the laying of hands and the massaging of her back. I added some prayer just to make sure. That eased the pain; but I didn't believe that it would eliminate the problem because she still couldn't settle down: so I asked her to roll over on her stomach. I placed the tomahawk on her back and asked for the white light while I whirled the crystal rod in a circular motion above her. Then I held the crystal rod in a vertical position, so that the blunt end was touching the tomahawk. Again I asked the universe for the white light to heal Cathy's back and to remove any negative energy. She was totally relaxed and the pain was gone after that.

The important thing is to believe in the powers of both the universe and your own self. Then you can't go wrong.

# 4.4 How to use your personal symbols in dreamtime

When we enter dreamtime, we enter the world of spirits and spirit communication. There are parts of your mind which the universe can tap into in order to convey bits of truth and teachings to prepare you for some of the unpleasant challenges which could arise from your actions or inactions. Travel in dreamtime is an opportunity to communicate with other levels of reality, receive teaching visions, travel in the spirit body and heal ones self or others.

One's personal visions and dreams can also provide one's direction on the path of life. Each of us is responsible for choosing our own life's path and each of us is responsible for interpreting our own dream symbols. Therefore, it would be a good idea to study symbols and the history of things to help you to understand the deeper meaning of your dream.

When you are in dreamtime: the past, the present and the future will become one; so it's important to understand that you have entered a timeless realm. Therefore the goal of dreaming is to bring your mental awareness into the picture, so that you catch the symbols without shattering the reality of dreamtime.

However, the interpretation of the dream is often done in the wakeful state after remembering the visions because it's often too difficult to teach a method of catching dreams and controlling the action at the same time. One suggestion is to place your symbol in the centre of a dream catcher, near your place of rest. Speak with the symbol repeatedly and remind it that you have the ability to choose your dreams. However, don't be frustrated with the results. Anything worth doing needs to be done over and over again until it works.

My dream catcher has the symbol of a medicine man in the centre of it. The spirit of the medicine man is also attached to it. Because of the difficulties in my previous home, the medicine man withdrew from my service. There were too many conflicts with the spirit world for him to cope with. In fact, the main reason he withdrew from me was because I was still dealing with my anger in the beginning. However, over time I was able to control that emotion. If I have need of him in the future, he will not refuse my request for assistance.

As with any symbols or strong personal beliefs, affirmations over time will bring you the requested results. If you request assistance from your guide because you are working on your spiritual development, your requests will not be refused. You need to imply that you have the ability to receive symbols from your dreams which will give you assistance. Then you will need to ask for the ability to control your dreams, so that you may achieve a higher level of awareness. If requested, your guide can also ensure that you will remember your dreamtime experiences upon awakening. Remember, all requests to your spirit guide should be repeated several times over.

Sometimes we choose to explore our inner selves and our souls. So those who are able to understand different aspects of the spirit world through their dreams should ask for further assistance; since they have been chosen to use their abilities in a more productive and rewarding manner.

# 4.5 Protective stones

Along with symbols, you will need protective stones and crystals. Protective stones are good to keep by you, if you are in haunted places or other negative areas such as doctor offices, courtrooms, police stations or bars.

Two of the best pendants you can wear are green jade and jet. Green jade stimulates the flow of positive energy within you and protects you against negativity. It is also a deterrent to sorcery and demonic possession. I keep a large Burmese double dragon at home for protection. It's the most expensive stone that I own; but it is worth it. You might say that the spirit of the stone has all the qualities of a chivalrous knight.

A jet pendant is also highly recommended because it is one of the most powerful amulets known. I keep a jet pendant on me most of the time because it can be used as a power rod outside of the home; plus, it absorbs negativity and assists the aura in healing.

A crystal healing rod should also be in your collection. A small rod may be carried with you, but a longer Atlantean power rod is best for clearing unseen intruders from your home. Mine has a six sided quartz point of clear crystal quartz which is wrapped in suede leather. It also has a copper wire wrapped around it.

Some other protective stones to keep around the house include: Aquamarine, Black Obsidian, Snowflake Obsidian, Smoky Quartz and Black Tourmaline.

# 4.6 When to take extra care

There are many books on chakras and how to keep the chakras in balance. When you are subjected to negative energies caused by surgery, accidental injury, x-rays or sudden shock for example; then you are vulnerable. If you are sensitive to energies, then you are also vulnerable to entity invasions.

Entities are capable of attacking humans and causing illness. If they can slap you on the face or push you, they will. They also like to attack the third and the sixth chakra areas.

The solar plexus is probably the most vulnerable area, since it is related to being happy and stimulated. If you strengthen and protect your solar plexus, it will give you power. If your solar plexus is vulnerable, you may be subject to stress, fear and anger.

The sixth chakra area is known as the third eye. It is between your two eyes; but slightly above them. If you are psychic and you are hit by a spirit in that area, you will likely experience temporary pain in your forehead.

Being pushed down the stairs from the top level is also a possibility. This has happened to Cathy on several occasions. Fortunately, she has survived all of them without an injury. I've been tripped a few times on the stairs as well. It doesn't hurt to be extra careful on the stairs in haunted places, since no one truly believes that a ghost can break your neck.

Moreover, entities and elementals can attach themselves to you, so it's better that you do not visit haunted places when you are sick, tired, depressed or you are not in control of yourself. Anyone who abuses drugs or alcohol should also stay away; since anything which weakens your aura will leave you wide open, unless you compensate with a strong believe in your powers. I would also recommend that you avoid insane asylums, mental institutions and prisons, if you are sensitive to negative vibrations.

*   *   *

Not surprisingly, entities will attack you at home when you least expect it. I had a long day at work and I was very tired one night. An entity took advantage of my situation and tried to attach itself to my back while I was in dreamtime. I felt my spirit being pulled back into my body; at the same moment, I was wide awake. At first, I focused on bringing the light into my self and my immediate surroundings. Then I realized that my aura had actually tripped my defensives and protected me, so that the entity was removed before it could even touch my body.

In some cases, fast moving, powerful entities can only be removed in dreamtime. For this you will need holy water. Either distilled or regular water can be converted. Put the water into a container and send energy into it through prayer and visualize the while light pouring into every molecule of the water. My technique is to hold the power rod in a vertical position and a glass of water in the other hand. The bottom of the glass is placed directly over the crystal point and the white light is requested. The white light will pass through the water on its way to the crystal.

Just before you are ready to go to bed, state your intentions of removing any entity intruders from your home and visualize the entity or entities, so they will be easier to track. Repeat the instructions at least twice and drink the holy water. You might want to wear a jet pendant and a Solomon's seal medallion for additional protection.

*Note: The most important step is to repeat this entire exercise again the next day. In addition, if you have a jet pendant wand close to you and an entity awakens you, you may use the jet as a power rod.*

In more serious cases, it will be necessary to use transformation in dreamtime to eliminate a powerful entity. Often we aren't allowed to remember our personal transformation dreams; but I have had the privilege with the permission of the Council, to view myself in my transformed state successfully take out some rather evil entities. The visions were so strong that my sons both witnessed and remembered my battles from their dreamtime.

# 4.7 Selected teachings on symbols and protection

**Amulet and talisman:** When you are away from home, your personal talisman or amulet can be programmed to help you maintain your personal force field and connect with the higher powers. Some consider an amulet to be protection while others consider the talisman to bring good luck. If you believe that a talisman or amulet can do something for you, then you are probably correct.

**Circle of protection (a useful power rod technique):** A power rod will always work; but it has to be aimed directly at the intended target; or the target has to be drawn towards the power rod's circle of protection. You can create this magnetic circle of protection by whirling the power rod clockwise, in a 360 degree circle. After several whirls, you will need to do a horizontal cut with the power rod (i.e., a swift movement with the power rod, along a 180 degree line in front of you), in order to remove the entity from your living space. (Note: It's better to use a second power rod for the horizontal cut maneuver).

**Crystal military formations:** For the following two defensive crystal formations, think of the 19th century British Army circle of protection.

> ➤ If you are using a crystal with a figure attached to it like an Indian chief for example and the crystal is small enough, place the chief crystal in front of the larger crystals.

> ➤ If the main figure; crystal; or crystal with a figure attached to it is larger; then put the main crystal; or figure, at the back of the formation.

Other protective formations with crystals include the:

- tomahawk formation
- arrow formation
- medicine circle

**Dreams of stone:** *Native American Indians have written much about the Red Road and the sacred Fire Teachings. "Dancing the Dream: The seven sacred paths of human transformation," by Jamie Sams (1998) is probably the definitive work on many aspects of this path. Other excellent books on sacred practices are "The Way of the Sacred Pipe," by Jim Tree, "The Sacred Pipe: Black Elk's account of the seven rites of the Oglala Sioux," recorded and edited by Joseph Epes Brown and "Breath of the Invisible: The way of the pipe," by John Redtail Freesoul.*

One can acquire perfect balance and harmony through the fire teachings and there is no need to go beyond them; nevertheless, there are mental perceptions and mystic ways which can be explained through formalized training. For example the "Dreams of Stone" (A.K.A. the Black Road), can teach us about living in spiritual darkness while seeking the light.

Chokecherry Gall Eagle in his book, "Beyond the Lodge of the Sun" stated something very profound about how people tried to put curses on his symbols and even tried to steal them because they thought they contained power. What happens to items which contain energy and are used for the wrong purpose by mortals is a topic which concerned Chokecherry more than evil spirits. Still, you can learn lessons from him.

He goes on to explain that you only have to reach down into your consciousness to throw the bad medicine off of you. In other words, bad medicine is not something which is inside you, it is something that is attached to you or put on you which you need to throw off like a smelly or foul blanket.

Other teachings from the Dreams of Stone:

> ➤ The search for meaning in our world begins with structure (the pipe, for example which represents a system of spiritual development); but the only way to the truth is through perception and consciousness (as represented by stone).

> ➤ Chokecherry states that when we go to the centre and seek unity (i.e., the centre of the medicine wheel, as indicated by the directional paths of initiation on the red road); then we will surly understand the symbolic meanings of all things.

> ➤ Chokecherry also suggested that your fundamental consciousness must be stronger than just a belief system. It must be a "truth of existence." Accordingly, the "dreams of stone" can teach us the way to transcend spiritual aids and ceremonial rituals, through perception and consciousness.

> ➤ In the end, we would be back where we started, in a more enlightened sense. There would be no need for religion; but the light would still be there for people to find.

**Grenadier drum and the bugle:** Regard signal instruments in emergency situations as the "shotgun approach" to tracking spirits. In the rare event of a "persistent assault;" whereas a spirit attacker retreats because of a power rod; then returns in *a more determined and aggressive manner*: the signal instrument can be used to subdue the attacker.

**Jet protection:**

- Place a sculpture of a grizzly bear (or some other protective animal) in front of a large brick size piece of jet. The jet should take its cue from the sculpture and from the other crystals in the vicinity.

- Some physical contact with each of your jet pieces on a regular basis is best; no matter how close in proximity you are to your household energy shields.

- You can also wear a jet pendant, carry a small jet piece in a pouch or a secure pocket; or hold a jet piece in your hand when needed.

**Military uniforms:** Clothes can be powerful: In particular, uniforms are protective. A uniform which is in good condition is best. Jacob wore a British 8th Army Redcoat to an 1812 re-enactment event during the fall of 2008. He charged at the enemy through some poison ivy and wasn't affected by it, as were some of the others. Was he was protected, or not from the poison ivy?

No one can say for sure; however, I was encouraged by the spirits to become a re-enactor myself; not because I really wanted to be one; but because the British 8th Army Redcoat that I selected would pick up the positive vibrations from the re-enactment events which I attended. In turn, the positive vibrations would give our home better protection and improve my luck.

Healing power is not a fantasy; since many re-enactors have had their luck change once they started going to these events. I also believe that both the re-enactor uniforms and the participants are "empowered with positive vibrations" from re-enactor activities.

I was also told to move the uniform around the house, since moving the uniform around the house breaks up the negative elements which have attached themselves to various items.

I even had to wear a suit at home for an hour each day and shine up some re-enactor equipment in order to keep things under control during the Christmas season a few years ago. As they say, if it works, don't knock it.

I have also found healing power at re-enactor scouting events; at special scouting ceremonies; and at large campfire gatherings, where scouting entertainments have invoked historical healing powers, related to the higher principles.

**Pictures and symbols:** Pictures and symbols which depict one's highest aspirations of life or one's dreams is a positive strategy to aid one's transition on the path to self-realization and spiritual fulfillment. A "dream shield" represents the circle of protection which surrounds our deepest desires. In some cases, a dream shield can also represent our higher self and the best things about us.

A circular dream shield can be a drawing with symbols, plants or animals associated with your dreamtime visions; or a 3 dimensional model with artifacts attached.

Suggestion:

- start with a medicine wheel which consists of four shields
- each of the four shields will depict an animal, a plant or some other aspect of the four directions
- colour and medicine can also be added
- create a dream shield which represents both your highest vision and your medicine power
- your chosen plant or animal, along with various symbols should become the dominant feature on the dream shield with crystals, rocks and other personal items hanging along the fringe of the shield
- remove pictures or items from the circular formation when aspirations, dreams or visions change, in order to allow for new growth

**Programming crystals:** The proper way to manage a crystal is to hold it, close your eyes and sense the energy aura in the crystal as it expands throughout your house and the area around your home. To program a crystal, you should exhale on the crystal, using three short breaths; then state your intentions after doing so.

**Sculpture and figures:** The Native American Indians understand the principle of oneness and spirit in everything, including inanimate objects. Accordingly, I have a great deal of respect for my large deer sculpture which has been carved into wood. The hairs on its mouth are real and the point of its nose acts as a power rod. It also receives positive energy through its antlers.

**Sending unwanted spirits to other places:**

Materials required: Use two crystal power rods.

Directions:

- The spirits can be drawn to the power rods by holding the two energy rods in front of you in a vertical position.

- The crystal power rods should be inclined towards each other with the crystals coming close together (you are forming two sides of a pyramid, or an inverted V shape). However, the crystals should not touch.

- Once the spirits are brought into your energy field, the two power rods are crossed in front of you.

- The two power rods are now crossing and forming an X shape (this formation is similar to the four directions).

- When the crystal rods are held in this position, the spirits will be sent to where ever you want to send them, for a specific period of time. You may also want to mention that they can never enter your premises again.

*A word of caution:* I had to debate with myself, whether to reveal this powerful technique. Please be careful what you ask for.

**Stones and crystals in copper bowls:** What happens when you create a heavy force field? You will probably increase spirit activity for awhile because the hidden spirits will be flushed out and they won't like it. This is what happened after I installed a few "household energy shields."

*   *   *

I could smell something bad upstairs after I placed a bowl of protective stones in the kitchen. Cathy cleaned the floors and the counter tops a few times, but it didn't help. So I got the crystal power rod and pointed it at everything, including the copper bowl of crystals. Before my eyes, something nasty appeared which happened to be the source of the problem. I won't say what it was; but it wasn't nice. Cathy and I had searched before; however, it was not visible.

*   *   *

The next day I was talking to Adam from the staircase. On the other side of the railing (on the upstairs landing), there was a walking cane. An entity intruder pushed the cane towards me in a threatening manner.

The following day our strongest cat was attacking something unseen on the main floor. He was jumping up and clawing at it. I ran up towards him with the power rod, but the spirit had already moved upstairs towards Jacob, who told me to "come up quickly with the power rod."

Cathy said that after I had dealt with the problem, the house had returned to a normal temperature much quicker than normal.

In brief, household shields can manifest positive changes, at a faster rate than stand alone crystals.

*Note: Sometimes cats will flag a spirit just before the temperature in the room changes. If you're lucky enough to have a cat on your lap when a spirit enters the room, you'll notice the cat's face look up and follow the spirit to its destination; since cats observe spirits like everything else.*

*   *   *

During the fall of 2008, I knew that I would be able to flush out the hidden entities and eventually cure many of the negative vibrations which remained in the house, if I were to place some protective stones in a copper bowl. At the very least the crystals in the bowl would work with everything else in the home. My first copper bowl of stones included a large jet egg, a super seven quartz point, a large black tourmaline, a Herkimer diamond, a purple quartz, moldavite, fluorite, pyrite, magnetite and black agate.

Afterwards, I decided to place a few more copper bowls around the house.

*Note: One should note that the size of the crystal isn't necessarily an issue when you are creating a household shield with crystals and a copper bowl. However, you should place at least one dominant crystal, egg or sphere in your bowl.*

*     *     *

I had been on patrols of the house for almost two years now and I figured it was time to try out the entire household shield network, as a stand alone; so I stopped the daily patrols. After three days, I was beginning to believe that I would never have to run around the house with the tomahawk again.

I had just come home from work on a nice cool October day and I was sitting on the couch near Cathy. That's when I felt the temperature change because of a cold blast of air. I went into the next room and I noticed that the A/C switch on the thermostat had been clicked on; plus, the lever had been pushed down to keep the A/C going for a long time. I had not used the A/C for over a month and I forgot to cut the breakers; so that was my first job. My second job was to go around the house with two power rods in hand.

Cathy stated that the spirits may have waited for me to get home so they could get my attention. They knew that if they turned on the A/C at that particular moment, they would have my attention and I would do exactly what I did. In fact, this incident was only the second time in three years that the A/C had been turned on since we had moved into our new home. I think a "friend" wanted me to go around the house in order to track another spirit.

There were less incidents of negative supernatural activity after the initial flushing out of entities with the household shields, except for a problem which was resolved on November 4th, 2008.

*Note: See the final entry in chapter two which was November 4th, 2008 (United States Presidential Election Day).*

# Part Five

## External Vibrations and Music

# 5.0 Psychic connections through external vibrations and music

Gongs, singing bowls, bells and other noise making devices have been used with chanting in many places in the world to intensify positive vibrations. The audible vibrations from church organs for example, appear to be stronger than most other instruments. I have used various vibration making devices myself to weaken the powers of evil, along with the signal bugle and the grenadier drum.

Some use mantras and other pure vibrations to alter their states of consciousness and to reawaken blocked channels. Mantras can also be used as a method of protection by restoring balance and reducing negative energies in the external environment. In brief, any energy which is created for healing, empowerment and renewed balance is positive.

There is also a word of warning for those who use sacred sounds for results. If the purpose of the music or sound is to empower you in an upbeat way; but you feel adverse to it; then perhaps you are exposing yourself to vibrations which are opposed to your own makeup.

Many years ago, both Cathy and I listened to a compact disc of Native American Indian songs which were intended to be sacred. The songs invited the spirits of the local natives to our home; but the results were different than expected. Cathy said that the natives who use to live in our locality were not in sync with us. She told me not to play the sacred songs again, even though the sacred songs may have been perfectly fine in a different area.

Another example of an external power is electromagnetic energy which permeates and surrounds our planet. The external vibrations from energy grids which bisect each other are called ley lines. Places which have been built on ley lines tend to hold emotional memories of the people who once frequented them.

There are other sources of external vibrations which should be noted. Crystal skulls have proven themselves to be beneficial for those who have heeded their call to action. Other inanimate objects which contain the previous owner's vibrations are not seen to be as powerful as ley lines and crystal skulls. Nevertheless, inanimate objects can carry both positive and negative vibrations which can impact on us. The vibrations which are attached to objects are basically tiny memory cells. They are also known as aka threads. If you are removing negative attachments from inanimate objects, you will need to replace the attachments with positive vibrations; otherwise more powerful energies can fill the void.

External vibrations can come from just about anywhere and can be imprinted on any article. You must use your own pure thoughts to activate the universal light force in order to erase the imprinted external vibrations which are not compatible with you; then you may fill in the vacuum with your own truth as positive vibrations. Placing your personal symbols around the object will also help.

The lesson here is very simple. On one hand, if you raise your own vibrations, you will be able to reduce spirit parasites who seek energy fields which may be related to the thought forms and vibrations which the spirits are most familiar with. However, when you are exposed to external vibrations in various areas and are not in alignment with them, the energy may cause unexpected problems. Accordingly, external vibrations can interfere with your conscious raising thoughts and may even encourage negative energies. In the event that you are confronted with powerful spirits, who are looking for a challenge or seeking new energy sources, just increase your awareness, so that your thoughts and your purpose are unified.

# 5.1 The aura and external vibrations

The aura is an electromagnetic energy field which does not directly depend on external vibrations for its source of energy; since it is a condition of all bodies. The aura is like your own personal force field which protects you from negative energy. It also contains a great deal of information about various aspects of your vitality, your mental state, your emotional well being and your spiritual understanding levels. It even contains colours which reflect the state of how balanced and grounded you are.

The outer shell, surrounding the aura, needs to be protected from undesirable thought forms and spirit intruders. This is especially true if you've depleted your energy because you've been exposed to negative situations. Negative thought forms can imbed themselves in your aura; therefore, letting go of negative thoughts is the best way to patch up any tears, cracks, or holes in your protective shell. Moreover, if you feel drained emotionally at any point in time, try visualizing your aura as a protective shell of positive energy which completely surrounds you.

Loving yourself, for what you are is the next step. If you accept what your intuition tells you, by loving yourself first; then you will attract the universal light force and increase your positive energy levels.

# 5.2 Trouble shooting with external vibrations

Natural settings usually work best because there is a pure resonance with the Earth. Nature has a unique way of healing, by revitalizing the mind and the body. Water soothes our vibrations and the sun gives us energy. The open air also gives us more awareness of our spiritual selves. If you resonate with nature, then all is well.

Being in a holy place has the same effect on many people. Nevertheless, we have met resistance in holy places. The first incident was in a church; the second incident was in the chapel at Fort Niagara which will be examined later on. (Note: Refer to 5.5). In both situations, the negative effects of external vibrations were turned around with positive energy. The positive turnaround at the church was due to the power of symbols and the turnaround in the chapel was due to Adam's music.

Cathy had visited numerous churches with the two boys one day in Toronto during an open house. She found all of the churches to be wonderful except for one. She found this particular church to be so negative that she couldn't look up. That was until she saw this beautiful window with an inscription which stated that the window had been given to a particular Canadian regiment, by the Cold Stream Guards. She felt perfectly fine after that and she no longer had any fear of anything in the church. Although it is possible that there might have been an unseen entity within the church, Cathy strongly believed that the negativity was related to someone who had visited the church earlier the same day. The external vibrations from that person or persons could have been left at the church. The cure was in the symbol because the church window resonated with her. For Cathy, the window was a symbol of protection. In brief, churches offer their own cures for what ails them.

# 5.3 The importance of sound in the spirit realms

In my opinion, the role of music in controlling one's personal environment and the role of sound in making connections with the higher realms are equally important. I found a copy of "Eckankar: the Key to Secret Worlds," by Paul Twitchell, as I was writing this book. I had written the date 1978 on Twitchell's book; so that is when I bought it. I remember my limited knowledge of the spiritual realms at the time; so it's unlikely that I picked up much from reading the book. The copy was still in good shape for a paperback, except for a large crack in the spine between pages 104 and 105. That is where I found most of the information which I required. Perhaps Twitchell's book had waited thirty years for me to understand the importance of sound in the universe in order to get a brief mention in this book; or perhaps a helpful spirit marked my copy of Eckankar just in case I didn't notice it for another thirty years. When the learner is ready, the teacher will appear.

According to Twitchell, the three essential principles for soul travel are thought, light and sound. The universal sound is the most important part of the three principles and it cannot be described in words. It is like a wave which flows from the Creator to every living thing in all universes. In this fashion, the light appears after the thought has take place which is followed by the sound. The universal sound wave is similar to the sounds of honey bees and is actually developed through the chakras.

It's resonance is also similar to the sound Hu. The drone of the sound Hu is a positive vibration which has been used in Gregorian chants, mantras, horns, flutes and other instruments as a means of raising one's spiritual awareness. Besides using the Hu sound for soul traveling, we can utilize it to bring out the best in ourselves and in the spirits around us.

# 5.4 Military music

The spirits at the historical forts have memories of their lives. They can be sad, angry or depressed and they can share their memories with living people as well, if we are open to them. However, some of their memories of war and battlefields can be frightening.

Cathy was getting some horrendous visions of British soldiers fighting during the Napoleonic Wars in Europe. She spent several nights on route marches with the soldiers in dry, arid places listening to the sound of the drums. In some cases, we all heard the audible sound of fifes and bagpipes in the morning hours which always stopped when you got up to investigate. This is what happened, as reported in the book Ghostly Allies.

August 12, 2006

We had gone down to Niagara-on-the-Lake for the day and we had just finished watching War and Peace at a very late hour. The video had some strong spiritual messages concerning the French Army's adventures in Russia during the early nineteenth century.

I was so tired that I fell asleep on the couch. About an hour later, Cathy woke me up. She was upset because she had been listening to fife playing for almost an hour. Jacob heard the lament too. They both thought it might be Adam; but Adam was fast asleep. In other words, the music was coming out of nowhere.

In the morning, Cathy asked Adam what the tune was. Adam had never played the tune on his fife; but he knew it. He said the mournful tune was called the Battle of Waterloo.

A few days later, Cathy heard some male voices in the morning while I was downstairs. Some of the terms in the conversation related to Spanish terms and the Napoleonic Wars. None of the terms were ever mentioned in the film War and Peace.

The night before we went to Fort George, Cathy had another vision. She described the night-time battle formation of two lines of soldiers and she felt that she was witnessing the action first hand. She could make out the white pants and red coats of the British and the bayonets. She said that the air was most unbelievably foul with smoke and there was screaming and cursing everywhere. She strongly felt there was some tie in with the Niagara area and the Napoleonic Wars. She told Adam about the name of the place called "Badajoz" which she heard the spirits talking about. Adam said that current day re-enactors at that battle site had become overly aggressive for no reason and had a go at each other. Are the dead at Badajoz still restless; or is it the battle site which gives off the aggressive vibes?

The siege of Badajoz took place in 1812 in an area between Spain and Portugal. The French lost about 1500 soldiers while the British lost about 3500.

August 25, 2006

I woke up early around 6:30am. I heard fife music and I was wondering why Adam would be playing so early in the morning. When I got up from the bed, the music stopped. Adam was sound asleep. It was another case of fife music which couldn't be accounted for.

September 9, 2006

Cathy had not been sleeping well because of her visions. The visions would start as soon as she put her head down to rest. Every time she went to sleep, she heard the beat of the military drum. She was part of a route march; but she didn't know why she was there. It was hot and dry. She could hear the soldiers talking about Badajoz again. When the soldiers weren't marching, they were drilling and practicing the standard British military formations of the time. This went on for at least three nights in a row.

September 12, 2006

Cathy was telling me how she had strong psychic connections with Spain. She knew nothing of Spain while she was living in England; yet she could draw magnificent Moorish pictures in her notebooks which accurately portrayed places she had never seen before. One of her teacher was so amazed with the drawings that she showed her work to the rest of the staff. Cathy really didn't know what the fuss was over until she saw a program on television a few months later that examined Moorish designs which she had no problem drawing from her own "imagination."

December 11, 2006

Cathy had a vision about a fortress, the night before. It had Moorish designs and it was the colour of sandstone. The main building was to the side of the walled fortification and the gate was wide open.

Cathy described the event as follows. She was with a group of people; but she couldn't describe them because she couldn't see their faces. She remembered approaching the fortress as the sun was going down. There was a body of water and a beautiful beach behind the fort.

The colours in this vision were quite vivid. The ocean and the sky were both deep blue. The sky turned a deep red, as the sun was setting. There were hundreds of lights all over the fortress. She said they looked like Christmas lights. She had a good feeling about the vision until she got inside the fort.

The paths within the fort were cobblestone and she noted that the Christmas lights were actually lit torches. She had a horrible feeling that she was walking into an ambush as she went up one of the narrow alleys. She felt that there was no escape or any turning back. She woke up and felt particularly bad about this vision for days on end because it was so realistic.

The vision could be tied in with a past life experience which needs to be re-examined in light of what has been happening in our current lives, or it could have been a spirit channeling his or her memory to us because of some personal connections from the past. There are spiritual healing methods in the universe which we have little knowledge of.

*    *    *

The following is an update.

Sometimes we need to use different tactics, other than the white light, symbols, candles, incense; or the use of powerful stones and crystals such as aquamarine, jade or jet. For instance, during the summer of 2008, I was playing a cat and mouse game with a spirit which appeared to dart away from several healing rods. It was making parts of the family room go hot and cold on an intermittent basis. Every time I did a sweep with the crystal rod or the tomahawk, it would disappear and reappear somewhere else. Rather then make a speech; I decided to use the bugle instead. The shrill attack call of the 19th century bugle eliminated the problem for the rest of the evening. The spirit world informed me many years ago that the grenadier drum and the bugle were both signal instruments which called on the forces of good.

*    *    *

Music appears to be a universal element that cannot be totally ignored in our psychic connections with the spirit world, since music tends to enhance the senses and stimulate recall. Harmonious, consciousness-raising music might have its place in meditating; but there is more to harmonizing with the spirits than harmonizing music. For those who simply want to reduce stress and strain in their lives, by all means listen to the tranquil variety. However, the following account has more to do with music preferences in the spirit world, than it does with the listener's preference for the same music.

The listener should be aware that I cannot reveal the identities of the spirit soldiers because of a promise. Their memories are honourable ones and the soldiers are still lead by an officer and a gentleman.

*    *    *

On this particular day in May of 2008, we had been visiting Niagara-on-the-Lake. We had hiked around Fort George and we had walked up to Fort Mississauga. We saw at least a dozen young people go into Fort Mississauga; but I refused to go into the fort because of the problems we had experienced there the year before.

We didn't notice anything as we walked away from the fort and back to the car. However on hindsight, one can easily conclude from this incident and from other visits to the forts that the spirits of soldiers are allowed to leave their posts, under the right circumstances. I now believe it's possible that we've carried spirits from the fort, on just about every occasion we've been in Niagara. The spirits usually return to the fort from our car or from our home, after a short stay. I also believe that most spirits who do leave the forts do not intend to cause problems. In fact, I believe that they have protected us from evil spirits on many occasions.

Normally Cathy gets a forlorn feeling of sadness when she leaves the Niagara area. On this particular trip homeward, Cathy, Jacob and Adam all felt extremely sad, as we passed Stony Creek on the Queen Elizabeth Expressway. Stony Creek is where the Americans were halted by British regulars, after the May 1813 invasion which destroyed both Point Mississauga and Fort George. Usually, we reach Burlington before the psychic feelings of forlorn sadness begin. But as we drive away from both Burlington and Lake Ontario, the feelings of sadness begin to disappear. Cathy believes that this particular psychic phenomenon is caused by the soldier spirits who have not gone beyond Burlington during their lifetimes and must return to their fort. In other cases, the spirits have something in common with us from a previous lifetime, or there is a personal interest which allows them to break free of their geographic confinements. These spirits are able to return home with us.

Adam usually plays military march music on the way home from the forts. On this trip, we had put on the radio and the radio hosts were playing some mellow classical music. We would have saved ourselves some bother if we had played British Grenadiers instead.

By the time we got home, Cathy was feeling extremely cold. It didn't look good; so I asked Adam and Jacob to help me out.

It was Jacob who captured the first lot of them with the commander. He knew exactly when it happened because the crystal power rod which he was holding became very warm all of a sudden. I knew we didn't have them all; but I told Jacob to follow me outside. Jacob told me that we must transfer the spirits from his power rod into mine before we went outside because they were too powerful. That should have been my first clue.

After we arrived at the back of the house, Jacob asked me where I wanted to send them. He suggested that it should not be any place in our local neighbourhood. I told him that I wanted them to be sent to Fort Mississauga. We both visualized Fort Mississauga and sent them on their way.

Jacob and I rushed back inside the house, where both Cathy and Adam were dealing with the remaining spirits. I started to do another monologue about sending the spirits back to Fort Mississauga, but Cathy told me to stop what I was doing. She stated what we needed to do instead. We had to play British Grenadiers on the stereo and then the soldiers would go back. She was in tears as she told me that quite a few British soldiers from the Niagara area had followed us home. However, all the soldiers who had followed us needed orders. Jacob had picked up the same message from the commander, who had just returned from Fort Mississauga. Moreover, Cathy stated that she was getting visions of soldiers leaving England before their arrival in Upper Canada, after seeing action in Spain during the Napoleonic Wars. She could also make out the uniform details of the soldiers. These soldiers appeared to be dressed in grey trousers, rather than the standard white ones.

The commander was still a bit angry; but he settled down after Adam played British Grenadiers. However, Adam played the orchestrated version and the commander told us that it did not have enough power to send them back to their fort. Adam got out his copy of some Fort George musicians who played the drums and fifes the old way. He played about ten or fifteen seconds of it. All of the spirits were returned to their fort, as a result of the music. It was quite an event. Although I sat rather stiff faced through the proceedings, the ordeal of the soldiers moved me. Cathy reminded me that releasing the soldiers from their earthbound status of guarding their fort could create a void with unforeseen consequences. I agreed with her. Although it goes against common wisdom, some theories of the earthbound appear to me to be too simplistic. In fact, I believe that Fort George is connected to a higher spiritual centre. I also believe that the forts in general are all in need of earthly healing power from human beings and that needs to be taken into consideration as well.

# 5.5 Haunted Fort Niagara

This is an excerpt from the audio book: "Haunted Fort Niagara" by R. G. Hilson. This account shows how music was used to defeat the negative vibrations in the chapel, during a visit to the French Castle.

*     *     *

After a short tour of the bottom floor, we climbed the thick wooden steps up to the second story vestibule. The barracks and the chapel came into view. The chapel; plus the top level were the two places which Cathy was mainly attracted to. There was also a sacristy behind the chapel; but it was not open to the public.

At first, the Jesuit chapel seemed very religious with an altar, a large cross and a Christ figure. Nevertheless, there was a strong negative presence within the room. We were captivated by the sacred symbols; yet, we were repelled by the spiritual forces around us. Reluctantly, Cathy was forced to leave the chapel due to the psychic negativity. Her forced withdrawal was also a personal disappointment given that she had been looking forward to this visit.

After we had visited all of the apartments and the officers' kitchen, there was still one more place to investigate. Cathy re-entered the second level vestibule. She walked over to the stairs and looked upwards towards the third level. Then she moved forward and climbed the stairs in a determined manner. We fell into step behind her like lemmings walking towards a sea cliff. There was no turning back now. Whatever had been waiting for her to return to the fort was up on the third level.

The third level was distinctly cooler. It was basically one large room; so you could easily see the entire third level. There was a ladder leading up to the roof and some well hidden loopholes which allowed fresh air inside. There wasn't much to see in the room itself, but everyone was very much aware that the third level environment was different from the rest of the castle.

Cathy tried to take a few pictures. The digital camera had worked everywhere so far, except when she tried to take a picture of the ladder. She tried five times without success. I focused on the ladder and imposed my will upon it. I told her that the camera would work. She took the picture. We reviewed our results on the camera's viewer. There were several visible orbs by the ladder.

By then, the psychic atmosphere of the third floor had begun to deteriorate significantly. Both the boys and Cathy were now aware of the oppressive nature of the third level. Adam got out his penny whistle which he had brought to the fort with him. He began to play the "Hanover Hornpipe." Things began to ease a bit. Not content with the first tune, Adam launched into a battle call, the "British Grenadiers." This tune was often associated with comfort and courage and has rallied the British troops for centuries. After the second tune, the malevolence completely disappeared. Adam had just finished playing the final note when he stopped abruptly.

Someone who worked at the fort had rushed up the stairs and had appeared at the top level with a ghastly pale look of fright about him. The expression on his face was of utter relief and his body seemed to relax after a half minute or so of tension. He said, "I thought you were," but he never finished the statement.

We knew perfectly well that he meant "ghosts." After the shock of seeing real people there, he admitted that he had heard the tune of the British Grenadiers from this place before. Obviously, there had been no one on the third level when he arrived the last time.

Then he apologized and seemed to be happy to leave the third floor. I asked Adam why he selected the "Hanover Hornpipe" and the "British Grenadiers;" since he knew how to play dozens of songs. He claimed that the sounds of each melody came into his head before he played them. As such, he strongly felt that the inspiration came from beyond.

Because of our success on the third floor, I felt that we should have another go at the chapel. I knew that Cathy would be disappointed, if we didn't try again. Adam played another tune upon entering the chapel. This one was called "Worship the King." This time Adam said that he had an even stronger feeling that he should play a particular melody. He claimed it was almost like a command.

It seemed like a miracle, but the chapel changed completely from a place of malevolency, to a place of joy and pleasantries.

# 5.6 Heavenly music

Among the early Christian writers, St. Anthony wrote: "We walk in the midst of demons, who give us evil thoughts: and also in the midst of good angels. When these latter are especially present, there is no disturbance, no contention, no clamor; but something so calm and gentle it fills the soul with gladness. The Lord is my witness that after many tears and fastings, I have been surrounded by a band of angels and joyfully joined in singing with them."

H. A. Baker also writes about the music of Heaven in his book: "Visions Beyond the Veil." He claims that the finest and the sweetest music found on the Earth is but a seeking for the lost chords and harmonies which the angels sing in Heaven.

Sylvia Browne states in her book: "Temples on the Other Side," that the angels are continually heard singing throughout Heaven. She also claims that the angels use a huge golden organ that emits a heavenly sound. I've been lucky to hear this heavenly choir and I believe that the lost chords and harmonies of Heaven keep things positive on the other side.

\*　　\*　　\*

Both Cathy and Adam love classical music. They also love listening to their recordings of various military marching bands. The recordings of the marching songs could be heard around the house constantly during the last eight months we were in our previous home.

I was lying down on the couch in the den one afternoon, when I heard music that I had never heard before. Right away I knew that this music did not come from an electronic stereo. The music was so emotionally moving that I couldn't budge. No human choir could reproduce the immaculate joy, sweetness and glory of those voices. I don't normally listen to any music unless it's background for doing my daily exercises; but I could have listened to that music for hours. The negative spirits would not have been able to handle the goodness that came from that sound. It would have washed away all of their dark intentions. I am positive that singing praise helps to keep negativity under control. I only wish the choir could have come back more often. I ran upstairs and asked Adam if he heard it too. Yes, he had heard the heavenly choir. It was all too brief. It was indeed the lost chord, or the holy grail of music.

After that we only experienced a few shorter episodes of heavenly music. However, when the choir wasn't in town, the stereo turned itself on without the benefit of a timer or human intervention. Perhaps the most unusual happening with the living room stereo was that Scotland the Brave would always play twice when we played a particular disc. Scotland the Brave was not at the beginning of the CD either, so there was no apparent reason for it, other than someone besides us, liked that track. Moreover, it didn't matter if Adam used his portable stereo on the dining room table or elsewhere. If he played the disc with Scotland the Brave on it anywhere in the house, the spirit would seek out that particular tune and the stereo would play the track twice. After we moved, everything went back to normal.

# Part Six

## Releasing Spirits

# 6.0 Releasing earthbound spirits with music

If the Creator decided to change the world in a day, He could probably just pipe down the music from the heavenly choir for every living soul on the Earth and all would be right with the world. That is why even the most perfect music on our planet is but a seeking for the lost chords and harmonies of Heaven. From the descendants of Adam who handled the harp and the organ (Genesis 4:21), until present day, all trumpets, organs, harps and other fine instruments are mere imitations of what they play in Heaven.

One might also expect that heavenly music could also be used against evil spirits.

For example, in the Old Testament, 1 Samuel 16:23, we read: "David took a harp, and played with his hand: so Saul was refreshed, and was well, and the evil spirit departed from him."

In Dr. Wickland's book, the spirit of Madam Blavatsky states that no matter how evil, how mean or how low a soul has become, they will still listen to music. Madam Blavatsky then goes on to explain how helping spirits can save souls. At first, the helping spirits concentrate on their targets. Then they play their heavenly music very softly, so that it can barely be heard. Once the helping spirits have the attention of their target audience with the heavenly music, the artists paint pictures of the higher life with little lessons and stories. Each set of pictures focuses on an individual's mistakes which encourages questions and more understanding of the higher life.

In spite of this valiant attempt to save souls, the spirit of Madam Blavatsky indicates that there are at least three groups for which the music and art strategy doesn't seem to work. The first is the religious fanatics' group: who sing, pray and praise a higher power. Apparently they are so hypnotized that no one can get through to them. The second is the misers' group. They are too busy counting money. The third and last group is the self-hypnotized. Many of these spirits were taught that death is nothing but an everlasting sleep. Nevertheless, the self-hypnotized group is probably the easiest one to turn around, according to the spirit of Madam Blavatsky.

# 6.1 Releasing earthbound spirits by example

If anyone believes in the "tough love approach," it must be John-Roger, who wrote Psychic Protection. He writes about a minister who was successful in eliminating entities from his entire church congregation only to have the entities return four fold within a short period of time. According to John-Roger, the minister's power began to back up on him because he was not creating a positive action. In fact, the reversal was having more of an impact on the minister's health than it was on his congregation.

When it comes to entity attachments, it would have been better for each church attendant to consciously work on their own behaviour and education. The minister could have supplied the universal light force and the congregation could have used that power individually as a method of regaining control of their consciousness. When you create a void, you must replace it with something positive of yourself. In the case of the unenlightened congregation, if you replace a negative with a negative, you get a bigger negative.

In brief, the best way to remove some entities is to use the light force as a direction finder in order to raise one's consciousness to a higher vibration. According to this method, the entity will move off by itself once it is sufficiently educated. The next step is up to the entity and the spirit helpers who are usually on the job.

# 6.2 Teaching earthbound spirits the higher principles by living in the now

One of the most important principles in achieving success in life is letting go, in order to make room for the now. It's possible that there would be fewer earthbound spirits if this principle was followed. There are many obsessions in life which keep spirits earthbound and perhaps we can learn about the Creator's will from this.

For some people, old desires, habits, dogmas, false teachings, indifference or disbelief in a future life can mean an earthbound existence. "As a man thinketh in his hearth, so is he." Prov. 23:7

Other spirits may remain in the environment that they once knew because of their strong interest or habits associated with their Earth lives. "Where your treasure is there will your heart be also." Matt. 6:21

Because many earthbound spirits get a rush out of struggling, or feeding their egos, perhaps we can learn to do the opposite. We should learn to let go and trust our intuition instead.

If you try to figure out all of life's answers ahead of time, you will surely limit both your thinking and your aspirations, since the conscious mind cannot see all the possibilities. It's like going down a river wondering what is around each bend. On the other hand, with patience your higher self can see everything clearly and set things up in their proper order. In fact, many people simply give up, if they can't come up with the right answers right away; then they listen to everybody else

Granted you might have to wait days, weeks, months or even years for something to go around. Your higher self will probably put you off and you'll wonder why you can't seem to get it together. Then when the time is right, everything will work out according to your soul's desire.

You should also be prepared; since the path to the truth may take you through some challenging territory. For anyone who is a leader or a teacher, there are admirers and foes on the sidelines. The good side helps us to deal with our challenges on this plane and the evil side wants to trip us up. Just know that you are perfection in God's eye; so that when you seek the truth from within, you will know yourself and love yourself as you are. This acceptance of your evolving spiritual self will also aid you in achieving purification which is the ultimate goal of spirituality.

# Part Seven

Heavenly Lessons

# 7.0 A heavenly lesson from John Lennon

With popular music, certain songs invoke negative energies. Even the Rolling Stones understood the concept of negative vibrations, when they stopped playing "Sympathy for the Devil" in their live concerts because of the problems the song created for them and everyone else. The words in that song were the obvious culprit.

In other cases, it's the singer not the song. This sighting on April 30th, 2008 did occur. As with any supernatural event, it is entirely up to the reader to interpret what happened.

\* \* \*

Jacob didn't know too much about the Beatles pop group. In fact he had heard very little of their music. Nevertheless, he was interested enough in them that he wanted to do a school project on the famous foursome. The project resulted in a couple of viewings of Yellow Submarine and a reading from an old book which I kept in the basement. Jacob had also seen the movie Help last summer.

Jacob and Adam had just finished lunch at home and Cathy was driving them back to school because they were a few minutes later than usual. Jacob had his Beatles' project with him in the car, since he had to present his work that afternoon. For some reason, Adam made an off the cuff remark about John Lennon.

Adam said that, "John Lennon thought a lot of himself."

Then the most extraordinary thing happened. They both saw a "man" on the sidewalk in front of them who was complete dressed in a shimmering white suit. The shoes, the tie and the suit were all white. Even his hair was white. Only the colour of his face was normal.

Both of the boys recognized the man as being John Lennon. John nodded his head at the two boys and let them know that he knew what they were talking about. Perhaps that was the biggest shock of all. Then he smiled at them and looked up at the sky. The boys looked at each other for a split second and looked again for the white figure. But John's spirit had already left them.

Even though the boys were talking about how unusual it was to see the spirit of John Lennon, Cathy could not see him. If anyone else could have seen him in our small town, they probably would have had a heart attack anyway. He was shimmering too much for the average folk in our area.

After I questioned the boys, they thought that John looked a bit old until they realized that his face was young enough, but his white hair made him look older. In fact he looked just the way he should look, except he couldn't make his hair look darker.

John's spirit is still with us to remind us of our need to stay the course, regardless of evil influences in our world. We are also very grateful to him for letting us know that our words and deeds do matter. Even though thoughts can take a long time to manifest in our dense plane of existence, our words appear to have more of an immediate impact; so we need to be mindful of what we say about others.

# 7.1 Lessons from the Heavenly Council

*"Men die, but are reborn in the real world of the Great-Hope, where there exists only the spirits of everything, and we are able to know this true life here on Earth if we purify our bodies and our souls, thus bring us closer to the Great-Hope which is All-Purity."* Hehaka Sapa, The Secret Rites of the Sioux Indians.

## Foreword

The narrator of "Lessons from the Heavenly Council" has collaborated with me over the past few years on several books which are related. The book Ghostly Allies introduced the Council and his mastery of life guardian. His mastery of life guardian (the Angel of Truth) also suggested to him that he should consider writing a book on eliminating negative energies. In fact, the writing of Ghost Tracker (an audio CD) and Shadow People were necessary soul tasks for the narrator.

The narrator, who goes by the name C.T. Shooting Star, thinks that many people are tempted to follow the sirens of the popular paths which are easy to find, but offer limited self-realization. On the other hand, he believes that this brief treatise will assist people in finding their own true path; thereby, experiencing the benefits of accelerated spiritual growth.

C.T. Shooting Star wants to thank both the Senior Council of Elders and his mastery of life guardian, by dedicating this new offering to them.

Yours truly,
R.G. Hilson

# Introduction

The day that my Ghost Tracker manuscript was sent to the publisher, my oldest son Adam was greeted by an evil looking, seven foot tall shadowy figure at the top of the stairs. He yelled downstairs for me. I told my son that the shadow entities were mainly fear mongers and nothing else. It was not surprising that this show of force resulted in the presence of angels, who also came to visit us later that same day.

Because of the spirit conflicts in our previous home, the Senior Council of Elders began to monitor my situation on a continual basis. But it was almost a year after the initial crisis before they got directly involved. The first thing they did was to appoint a mastery of life angel to be with me on a daily basis. I was given his specialty title and his personal name. All I had to do was ask for him and he would be there with me. In the beginning, he would offer me advice and a plan to deal with the high level of difficulties that I was facing at home. After things settled down, he would appear on an ad hoc basis. Later on, I found out that he had always been my guardian and that he would be with me for the rest of my life.

Based on my personal experiences with the divine, I believe that the main obstacle on our human path way is fear. It's time that we put our fears behind us. The mastery of life angels are available to work with us, so that we can complete our necessary soul tasks and achieve our spiritual goals. The Council of Elders and the Creator are also fully aware of how far along our individual paths we have traveled. The most significant realization of all is to discover that we are never alone, as we make our way along the spiritual path.

## Interpreting fear in our dreams

Facing your fears is a key part of your spiritual growth. Since you will have to face your greatest fears eventually, it's better to turn around and face them, than to have them follow you around like a dark shadow which appears to grow in intensity to your self-made fears.

One of the best ways of dealing with fear is through dreams and visions. I was accosted by bats in my visions very recently. I turned around and bit the bats! Turning your fears around may work in the dream world; however, you still need to interpret your visions before you can place any value on them. Your visions should be analyzed in accordance with the actual events which take place after the visions have occurred. For example, the bats in my visions may have appeared as fear; but the bats as symbols could have been interpreted as rebirth.

Just after my visions of the bats, I began this audio book on rebirth and spirituality. Related to the notion of rebirth, the bats visions could also have set up a series of problem solving exercises which gave birth to a manuscript. Because there is duality in dreams and symbols, you should remain open-minded until the true meaning of your visions can be understood.

The practice of discernment is in fact our greatest challenge. Don't judge the symbol on how you react to it; just learn something from your reaction and be open to different interpretations. There is no right or wrong. It's just part of our spiritual duality.

## Journey to the past

It's never too late to start working towards the divine. In order to know how far you've come and how far you still need to go, you may need to re-visit the distant past. My destiny was to re-visit one particular identity. I was told the truth about this identity, not once, but a dozen or more times over a period of years. Even when I moved to another home, I contacted my guardian angel and the information was backed up again.

In the beginning, my guardians prompted me to ask questions about my North American native lifestyle. Then they encouraged me to obtain a few native artifacts, a peace pipe tomahawk and a copy of the Last of the Mohicans.

The tomahawk was important because it had special spiritual attributes. Its main function was to generate positive energy. As a healing weapon, it also helped me to create a bond between my current life time and my past self.

\* \* \*

Fort George in the Niagara region of Ontario was chosen for me to be my spiritual base. Other historical forts which I have visited have also given me spiritual energy related to Karma. When visiting Fort George, I can bring healing to the lost souls who are attached to the past and they in turn can give energy back to me. I've been told that many spirits would seek me out if I did not visit Fort George on an annual basis. Sometimes the spirits of the fort visit me regardless.

There are several reasons why the spirits of the dead soldiers move on to the next life and there are just as many reasons why they remain. Visitors to the forts, who honour the sacrifice which these soldiers have made, are usually welcomed. However, if you are sensitive to psychic phenomena, you might experience negative energy at some of the historical sites. Battlefields which have memorials; but no graveyards or re-enactor soldiers, appear to be more negative. Based on my family's experience, Queenston Heights, Fort Mississauga and Chippewa are the most negative sites in the Niagara area, related to the War of 1812.

\*    \*    \*

Learning from the past is important, but how you learn is an individual matter. I was told many of my identities and I was comfortable with the knowledge. I also felt that I had resolved many of my own issues without the need to find the source. But because of the spirit events which I was faced with, I sought further understanding of my destiny from my guardians.

The Creator allowed the Council to reveal my North American native identity as mentioned, but I was told more. My two sons and I joined the British side during the War of 1812. My eldest son was an officer of high rank and he died early in the conflict. The youngest one was a junior officer. He was the only one of us who survived the war.

Because military conflicts have taken a huge toll on my past lives in the last two hundred years, the message I want to pass on to you is this. The War of 1812 Karmic cycle is almost over for me; however, it took almost two hundred years to resolve some of my Karmic issues.

If you feel that there is something from a previous life time which is blocking your soul development and you want to correct it; then you have a few options. Regression to a previous life time is possible; but you may have several identities to work through. Before you consider using regression, you might consider getting your information directly from the Akashic Records. The Akashic Records contain all the information for every individual who has ever lived upon the Earth. The record captures every word, deed, thought and intent that has ever occurred. The supervisors of the records will also be able to help you zero in on your current needs.

Alternatively, you can get help directly from your guardians, since they are in contact with the Council. Just remember that the Council does not deal with frivolous entertainments; so it is imperative that you respect their teachings, if you are given anything to work on.

# Fulfilling our purpose

The purpose of life is to know the Creator. There is really only one common life force that exists as love and that pervades all living matter. The Creator is the force of the universe and the pervasive unity of life that is in all things.

To know the Creator, we have to understand that separation is an illusion. Our souls are of the Creator. To experience the soul's purpose is to connect with our previous lives in harmony, with others and with the divine.

The soul knows its true purpose. In a struggle with an individual's ego or personality, the soul will win. Because the soul works to manifest its destiny in a life time, the struggle and effort of resistance may end up in a crisis at some point. For example, a disease or an injury can bring focus to the ego; so that the individual can proceed with the work that they were intended to do. Another example is when people ignore community concerns; but in times of crisis, they pull together. This is also part of the divine plan.

The planning of a rebirth is a big job. Much effort goes into it; since many of your family members are involved. There will be different roles to choose from. One of my family guardians appeared to be eager to suggest some creative options for my next life time. In fact it was one of my female guardians who suggested that I might want to come back as the opposite sex. I have a suspicion that I have never been a female, based on what I know of my soul's journey on this planet. Being a female invites different experiences and that might be something that a soul requires. Still, there are many paths and there are many ways of achieving our life's experiences.

Other souls depend on the success of your life time; so it is important that the lessons which were planned for the journey are fulfilled. The only way to accomplish one's destiny is to live life to the end and to pay attention to whether you are content with the status quo.

Even with all the planning before time, you still have the freedom to choose a different path. My family has been together three times before in the same roles, except for one of my relations. There was a change there. Because of free will, some things in our world don't always go according to the divine plan.

In the future, our divine messengers may take more of an active role in our destinies. Both of my sons were taught several formalized ceremonies and how to program crystals. They were barely out of kindergarten; but they took to the spiritual realm like it was second nature. As adults, we forget and we simply don't want to know. The material world becomes our reality and the spirit world becomes a distant memory.

## Our spiritual challenge

To arise out of the self-created fear, the darkness and the separateness is to embrace the truth and the power that you are and that which is within you. Abundance or the highest prosperity is achievable when you follow your heart and live your dreams. All that which exists is fed from the Tree of Life. Having eaten from this tree, means that you are blessed with both a life force and a soul that are eternal. Therefore, one should honour the Creator's gift of life with gratitude.

However, eating from the Tree of Life also means taking fear into you which results in ego or a separate idea of self, from which self springs. Once fear is manifested, the communion with the Creator is broken and you are literally cast out of paradise. Therefore, the goal of the human path is to return to the divine through the experience of knowledge. Knowledge means knowing yourself as a separate being with importance.

Related to the power of Karma and energy returned is the creation of a place which we like to call Hell. Those who exist in a state of hell are really in a state of separation and disconnect with the divine. Fear is the predominant life force in Hell. From a Karmic perspective, Hell creates a life force of fear which is self-perpetuating and self-fulfilling. It expands and then it builds upon itself.

Even though all of creation is in perfect harmony, there is total flexibility of free will to make decisions, chose actions and to follow a specific path or none at all. One can either chose to succeed or fail in their life's purpose, even after being chosen to complete a specific purpose or to accomplish specific things. The real spiritual challenge is whether or not you can accomplish it. I was told that many had been chosen for the path that I was on and most or all, had failed. Eventually they told me that I would win, when things began to look hopeless. Persistence is the key to success.

# The end result is purification

Purification is how you view things and whether you can make the necessary changes within yourself. Therefore, the purpose of purification is to learn the truth about yourself and your surroundings. There are things in life which you can't change; at the same time, you still need to address the situations which you can change. In both situations, be open to your thoughts and feelings. Address the necessary changes which you need to make within yourself and accept the changes.

The more you understand everything about yourself, the easier it will be to purify your communications and your feelings. Total purification is the end result of spiritual discipline.

# How to improve spiritual discipline

Our path appears in the silence when we become more aware of our thoughts and our feelings. When we realize that there is a connection between the unseen world and ourselves, there is more clarity yet. Some people begin to connect in spirit form with the universal force while sleeping and dreaming. Others use meditation. Once we realize that we can create matter by putting out energy into the universe, we can take control of our destinies by choosing the right way which is uniquely ours. Karma is a potent force when you place energy into the universe. That energy is returned in a more powerful form, providing greater opportunities for the soul to grow. Then it becomes a case of persistence in whether we obtain what it is that we desire.

No one can tell you how to find your own unique path because the true quest on any spiritual path is to find the desired spiritual growth directly. Religion can provide a path by giving one an intellectual understanding of what they seek and a spiritual understanding. However, religion relies on others' inner knowledge which they have gained from their higher self or from the angels. Even the best information available to you from others will always fall short of what you can attain through inner knowledge.

One of the greatest difficulties is the practice of discernment. Discernment is whether the thoughts you have, or guidance received is a form of higher vibration which will guide and direct you in a healthy and positive way. If the guidance you seek is based on love rather than fear, then it is probably the true path.

Often you will only proceed in a new direction when you are ready. In other words, your higher self will only challenge you when the time is right. You may have to proceed in ways which appear to have no connection to your desires in the beginning. The key is to consider everything that comes to you, no matter how inconsequential you perceive it to be. Just pay attention to any feelings of joy in your heart. That is also part of the discernment process.

Many people give up easily on a task when they run into resistance. This can be caused by a lack of support, people not agreeing with you and those who might try to prevent you from accomplishing your task. Often the struggle comes from your own mind which means that all of the negative and limited thoughts which you have are really at the heart of why you are dissuaded, prevented or blocked from completing your task. This kind of behaviour contributes nothing to your soul development. On the other hand, a person who is stubborn and refuses to give up can also be at odds with their soul's journey. They go against the flow despite all of the warning signs of fatigue, until finally there is exhaustion and collapse. Every individual needs to judge the difficulty verses the ease of each task, in order to know whether they are in alignment with, or in opposition to the flow. It's a key spiritual skill to know whether a difficulty is an opportunity for growth, or whether it is a signal of misdirection. Discernment is in fact the key to all great spiritual growth through human life because each human path is unique.

# Walking

Walking helps to improve spiritual discipline because physical exercise provides a means of achieving purification of and control over one's thoughts, feelings, words and gestures. Walking also reinforces the truth that a simple and natural approach is best and through walking we can discover this.

In our previous home, I had to deal with a demon who knew how to use telepathy. I was forced to consider strategies other than fighting. My senior level mastery of life angel told me that I must walk for several hours each night in sub-zero temperatures in order to find the balance I was seeking. The balance I was seeking can be described as alert relaxation which is the same as the feeling that you get when you are doing well at something and feeling confident in yourself while at the same time, you are not overly concerned with the outcome of your perceived conflict.

Walking not only gives you good health, it makes it easier for you to relax your mind and body while you are dealing with conflict. Walking is also a vehicle which gives you more focus and coordinated power. When participating in any mental or physical activity the principles are the same.

Lasting spirituality comes from what we find in our everyday lives and our routines. We need to use routines to condition ourselves to repeat certain acts that we can grow from everyday. However, the feelings that we get from within as a result of the act must never become boring. For example, if a particular walking route becomes boring, then change your route to a more natural place with many living things. Whatever route you choose, just be prepared to get into a state of harmony with everything around you which might include cars, dogs and other people. In this way, you must be in a state of relaxed alertness.

# Meditating

Meditating in a quiet place and thinking about your thoughts is a strategy for spiritual discipline and for achieving purification. If you can change your perception to become more whole; then it will be easier to purify yourself even under the most troubling circumstances. Moreover, if you meditate with the correct mind-set, you will gain more control over yourself.

It's best to sit with your spinal column towards the sky. The extra energy which is normally used when you do everything else will become a positive force inside of your being. This positive energy will revive you and improve your mental well being.

If you have strong feelings about something, or your feelings about something appear to be changing, then you want to see what is influencing your change in direction. Sometimes a decision is made without sufficient knowledge and a mistake is made. It is better to think about why the mistake was made and to make the necessary change.

If you don't wish to own the problem by thinking bad thoughts about someone or something, you need to work on a sense of detachment. If you can't be neutral, you still must be non-judgmental. That means applying the opposite thought to whatever bad thoughts you are thinking. In other words, by separating the thoughts which only you can influence, you can apply the opposite thought to the things which you find are negative.

# What transparency teaches us about fear

Meditation also helps you to become more transparent, so that you won't make any judgments about others' behaviour. The first step is to keep your emotions intact by acting from a calm, clear centre. One of the best ways to become transparent is to find some aspect of others' behaviours you can harmonize with. If someone is too low of a vibration, simple take your focus off the situation and tune into a higher frequency. If you are not able to take the higher path, then there is likely an element of fear present.

One of the interesting aspects of reacting to peoples' feelings is that they would not annoy you unless you had similar feelings, attitudes or behaviour; however minor, yourself. When they act in ways that you don't appreciate, they are mirroring back to you a part of yourself that you haven't yet learned to love. Learning to love every aspect of yourself raises your vibration and no longer attracts a lower vibration which you no longer want to attract. By mastering your fear, you will probably recognize that specific fear in others; but you will no longer feel their fear as if it were your own. Then you can feel peaceful, calm, centered and balanced no matter who is around or what is happening.

## Becoming more centered

Meditation will also help you to become more centered. Centering is an elevated state of consciousness which occurs when all the attributes of one's consciousness become focused on the here and now. Centering can be described as being calm amidst the swirling flow of life. Imagine that a stream is comprised of time, water, wind and manifestation. You stay in the middle of the stream fully centered, standing on a strong foundation of natural stone. When you are centered, you are also in a state of alert relaxation and symbolically placed above the material realm. You can still fully enjoy the pace and changes in the material life, but you are no longer consumed by it, unlike many others who appear to bounce from one side of the stream to the other. Instead, you adopt and manage your own desires, based on your own needs.

## Staying in balance on the right path

Listening is a key skill which will help you to stay in balance. If you hear negative discourse in your social interactions, then you should ensure that you maintain your own viewpoints of harmony and not adopt other viewpoints, just to be accepted. Then you will be in a better position to balance the conversation by adding a positive to any negative statements being made. If the person is an enemy and you change a negative thought to a positive, you'll gain even more energy.

You should also pay attention to how much you give and how much you receive from others. It is okay to help people, to help themselves; but you'll need to focus on your own energy levels foremost. Those who take advantage of your good will deplete your energy levels and hinder your forward progress. You cannot feel responsible for everyone's happiness. Only they can choose it for themselves.

If the return of your thoughts and feelings, related to balance is out of sync; then one might expect imbalances related to health, attitude, emotions, psychological well-being, spiritual purpose and even a feeling of separateness.

# Advanced spiritual development

Non-attachment accelerates one's spiritual growth because it allows you to achieve a higher harmony with others and by doing so you are also free of any ego struggles. Releasing the things that no longer serve you, blessing them as they leave and embracing the new is necessary. Everything comes into your life to teach you something. When a person, situation or thing has taught you all it can, then it is time to replace it with something else which will provide new opportunities to grow. One of the most difficult attachments to let go of might be your viewpoint, your beliefs or your judgments. You are always being challenged by your higher self to think in new and expansive ways. By the same token, you are not responsible for making other peoples' lives work; they are. In fact, the need to save people from making mistakes will slow your own growth. Whenever you help someone, you give them whatever assistance they require as viewed from your higher self, then you need to detach from the outcome. One of the greatest gifts you can give someone is to allow them the freedom to go their own w ay.

While maintaining your own spiritual discipline, be mindful that there are others who need to learn lessons too. When you get involved with someone else's Karma, it becomes your Karma too. Many other people will be impacted, including the person for whom the thoughts are directed, before they are returned. Therefore, consider using the power of judgment and actions to create Karma based on love rather than fear; since the judgment of others creates Karmic energy based on fear.

# Becoming a spiritual warrior

A spiritual warrior is someone who has stopped looking for external enemies and has turned to face the enemies within. Shifting one's perspective means that the warrior must be brave enough to go the distance and be prepared to strengthen their weaknesses with positive strategies. When we are putting ourselves forward and facing our greatest adversities, we are learning to heal the past and all regret, showing no fear of the future and focusing on being aware and fully present, all of time. Ultimately, we walk away with the knowledge that all life is connected in some way, shape or form. Moreover, there are no answers outside of ourselves; since we are already connected to all universal truths.

If you are pushed into an emotional or physical corner by a worthy opponent, keep working towards purification. You can gain both wisdom and accelerated spiritual growth from a worthy opponent because you are forced to make changes. A worthy opponent is the true test of who you are and how you use the tools of your spiritual path.

Those with opposing values make Earth the best school possible to learn lessons; but one of the most difficult tests of all is when your opponent is perceived to be evil. Evil is the Creator's love filtered within the human consciousness; so it's important to remember that balance always returns to the universe and healing occurs when it looks like the evil side is winning. Ultimately, only fear can block your communion experience with the divine; so you have no choice but to traverse the fear itself, no matter what challenges you are given.

I've had many such challenges with evil; but it always comes down to the same thing: the intensity of the challenge and the duration. The intensity is the shock factor and the duration of the challenge can result in burn-out. If you are involved in soul evolution, the Council has a good idea of how much you can take, since the lessons you chose were selected in collaboration with them. If you've bitten off more than you can chew, the Council won't let you down, if you ask for their help.

I now leave you with my final thoughts on spiritual development. This is a time of shifting, so there is a need for more enlightenment, to accomplish many things. Believe in the powers of the universe that are within you and around you, regardless of your difficulties along the human path, or how well things appear to be going for you. Be open to receive and seek the truth from within. Encourage others to be all that they can be. Most of all, give many thanks to the Creator for your eternal soul.

# Part Eight

## Maintaining a Light Fortress

*You may ask: what is a light fortress? The answer is: all that which contributes to your truth. In other words, whatever you are working towards right now, contributes to your truth. Ultimately, your light fortress will be different from mine. Suggestion: You might want to start with parts of the Bible for your cornerstone.*

# 8.0 Creating a foundation for a light fortress

The Bible is the cornerstone. Many people might suggest that the Holy Bible is also your first line of defense. That's what I thought too. When I was told by a powerful spirit that he would be moving into my house and ejecting me from my own office, the first thing I did was place my grandparent's Holy Bible on the top of my desk. Within five seconds, the sacred book was tossed onto the floor in front of me. Evil knows no bounds.

The Bible may not be your first line of defense; but it does contain important information which will help you to create the foundation of your light fortress.

The Sermon on the Mount (Matthew 5,6,7) provides some of the most crucial information for our purposes and the purposes of good. But before one can effectively defend yourself against powerful evil forces, you must be pure in heart.

> And the rain descended, and the floods came, and the winds blew, and beat upon that house; and it fell not: for it was founded upon a rock.

> (Matthew 7:25)

To create a foundation of rock, one can look to the Lord's Prayer for guidance.

Our Father which art in heaven,
Hallowed be thy name.
Thy kingdom come.
Thy will be done in earth, as it is in heaven.
Give us this day our daily bread.
And forgive us our debts, as we forgive our debtors.
And lead us not into temptation, but deliver us from evil:
For thine is the kingdom, and the power, and the glory, for ever.
A-men.

(Matthew 6: 9-13)

Repeating the Lord's Prayer on a daily basis will also help you to enact the powerful forces of good; but more importantly, the Lord's Prayer is a cornerstone of the good which you can create for yourself.

# 8.1 On choosing higher principles

During the spring of 2008, I was listening to the local CBC station in Toronto while I was driving in an open area, a quarter of a kilometer north of Toronto, so there was no way I could have lost my station. However, a spirit changed the station for me and I heard the following biblical quotation.

"For God so loved the world that he gave his only begotten Son, that whoever believeth in him should not perish, but have everlasting life."

The quotation from John 3:16 startled me so much that I changed the station back immediately, until it dawned on me that I was to use the quote in this book. I thanked the universe and promised to do so.

I should add that Christ taught us to honour God above all else. Christ also said that we should also live our lives according to his high principles, as the true understanding and the light of life. Personally, I have the highest respect for Christ because of his fearless ability to stand up to the forces of evil.

# 8.2 Human evil as a catalyst for evil spirits

What is the role of human evil in our lives? Unfortunately, religion has failed to understand the nature of evil. Perhaps we should turn to Shakespeare, who understood human evil better than anyone. He stated that the evil that men do lives after them.

Evil creates more evil. After awhile it becomes a vicious cycle which has no beginning and no end. I also believe that man has the means to stop it cold, but most men seek the answers outside of themselves which often leads to other men who are of the same mind.

Many follow a path of corruption because it's easier to do so; or they have lost faith in themselves. Yes, I see corruption only too clearly. Nevertheless, branding human beings as evil is a risk taking business best left alone.

If you can't avoid human evil, you can at least neutralize its influence. There are five points to consider.

- Use your strengths to combat negativity and achieve self-realization.

- First discover; then choose appropriate lessons to be learned which you think can help you get started towards self-discovery.

- Have faith in your spiritual evolution.

- Renew your faith often.

- Remember everything you need for the journey is already in place.

Also, don't worry if it looks like you're not pulling your weight in life. Every path is different. Because we are all here on this planet for different reasons, we also contribute to the welfare of our fellow man in different ways.

# 8.3 Psychic protection

The ancient kings were buried with their jet pieces for two reasons. They knew that jet contained protective powers. The ancient kings also knew that jet should only have one owner.

A jet pendant is handy to have on you when you don't want to attract attention to yourself. If you are outside the home, I would recommend a jet pendant which can be worn around your neck or inserted in a sealed pocket.

In situations where you need to neutralize negative psychic phenomena, the pendant can be produced and held in one's dominant hand. If jet is used as a light weapon, it can have the same effect on negative energy as a power rod. In terms of dealing with spirits, a light weapon is considered to be a healing strategy.

Also, please do not underestimate jet. I've seen jet literally jump into action against a negative spirit. One time, I saw my pendant disappear from Jacob's hand after a spirit was eliminated. The jet returned to my sealed shirt pocket after Jacob said that it was now in my possession. Jet is definitely the most aggression protection that you can find, if you need that kind of protection.

There are other more subtle techniques which offer protection against negative energy. The stomach and the heart chakra regions for example, are areas which you intuitively protect when you're not sure of your environment.

Your auric circle should be reinforced in the event that the pure clear white light protection which already surrounds you is weakened by disease, an injury, an unhealthy environment and or an emotional shock. Being around haunted places can also cause your auric circle to weaken. In other words, if you are already under stress, you may have to work harder at maintaining your personal force field.

One strategy is to use imagery. Imagine that the force field around you which protects you and keeps your chakras in balance is like a big egg or an oval shaped sphere, with you inside of it. Also imagine that the outside shell is made of positive energy which neutralizes the negative. In fact, the auric circle should provide your best line of defense in most situations. The jet will also back you up when you have need of it.

Circles of protection aren't news to the spirit world either. Orbs are spheres; but they are also act like protective circles of light. Cathy saw a spirit emitting bright light beside her desk one day. She described the spirit as being an elongated oval sphere. She also captured an amazing digital picture of a huge oval sphere in front of the Christmas tree when she was feeling low one day. The image of the bright white sphere covered seventy-five percent of the picture. We strongly felt that the spirits in both cases were guardians.

# 8.4 Becoming a light warrior

*The transition to the warrior level of protection is significant, if you are ever forced to fight malicious entities and win on the first round. If the warrior's soul is true to his or her purpose of being free from unwanted negative energies and has peaceful intentions, then the ULF (Universal Light Force) will be effective. Since ULF strategies only seek out negative energies and do not affect those spirits and energies which are of the light, many ghostly allies will gladly aid you in your personal fight against negativity and in the spiritual transition to light warrior.*

There are three levels of "transition to light warrior" in my opinion. Under adverse conditions, a light warrior must pass through all three stages.

Being a light warrior also comes with some strong medicine. The light warrior approach to protection is only for those who want to take full responsibility for their total being with help from their higher self and their spirit guardians. These techniques are not desirable for those who are not willing to look after themselves, since these techniques will test your faith in the universal power.

The first test for the light warrior begins when he or she has to identify the psychic phenomena. In our world, if you identify a group of people as evil just because others think they are, it's possible that you might be falling into a trap. For example, I've already indicated in my accounts of ghostly doubles and ghostly cats that nothing negative occurred in either case. However, in other case studies which I've read, if you see your double, then something very bad will happen. In fact, I've read that if someone else sees your double; then something bad will happen also. Fortunately for me that has not been the case. Or did I just get lucky?

Some of my favourite books by Elliot O'Donnell contain these bad luck stories; yet, I would prefer not to be stricken by fear because I believe the first test is that you must not give into fear. In brief, if you are already being influenced by negativity or group think, then you may fail the first test.

The second test is to know the truth. This is important if you want to neutralize the influence of the evil spirits. If you believe the lies, you will not be able to eliminate anything. This can be the most frustrating and pain staking test of all. You know in your heart whether something is right or not. You must apply the same principals of right and wrong towards your adversaries. Powerful spirits will fake their identities, or they will use fear to weaken you. Be aggressive and firm with them. If they are not of the light, then in the name of the Creator, they are not welcomed.

The third and final test is taking action. I use an Atlantean power rod which contains a special crystal. The crystal healing rod is wrapped in suede leather and has a heavy copper wire wrapped around it. Your main healing weapon should be held in your dominant hand. The crystal rod works in a similar way as a pyramid. The energy is stored within the rod and is amplified by the crystal. With practice, the energy you create can be unlimited. You can visualize it and you can create it by whirling the rod in a circular motion, much like a coil of energy from the chakra which is effective in manifesting positive energy. For those who are practiced in imagery, a pyramid in front of a coil of energy can also produce matter.

For extra power, I rotate the rod at the heavens above in order to place white light around the house or to flood the inside of the house with the light, since the intruders are already inside. My only goal here is to make it uncomfortable for them and force them out. While I am doing this I am also asking for protection for the house and all those who are in it. Nevertheless, this extreme tactic often invites retaliation from powerful evil spirits who can slip in and out of a house. In some cases, it leaves an instance void. Just repeat the routine within five minutes and any potential revenge attack will be quashed.

# 8.5 Medicine power

There are millions; perhaps billions of stars in the universe; one for every human being and perhaps more. Some even say that each star has a soul. When man looks to the stars, his glaze is full of wonder and his heart yearns for the truth. Man's search for meaning may take him to the stars; but it is the theme of "finding one's destiny" which often determines our success or failure in this lifetime.

Perhaps one of the most popular films of all time was "Lost Horizons" which looked at utopia as being a place where individuals could share a destiny and live on happily together. Other attempts at utopia have been made; but for many classic film enthusiasts, Lost Horizons is probably the best example. If a man could live forever in Shangri-La, or at least to a ripe old age; perhaps he would gain enough wisdom to live the life he ought to live.

But what if there was more to life than just one lifetime and as a result, relationships were not lost through the centuries. Accordingly, would it not be possibly for family members to be reunited in different lifetimes and in different family relationships? This notion also suggests that historical figures with strong relationships in the past could also be reunited in the present, as family or friends because they chose to be reunited.

Individuals may choose experiences, according to their soul's desire or learn lessons "the hard way." Knowing your previous identities is somewhat helpful, but not necessary, since following your intuition is all that is required. Family members are not only reunited in different lifetimes, they also act as guardians to the living.

I went to a Native American Indian fortune teller many years before. He told me that my unborn daughter was always with us.

At the time, it was just about the most unsettling thing which I had ever heard. It wasn't until many years later that Adam had a dream in October of 2007 in which the prediction came true. The spirit in Adam's dream introduced herself as his older sister. Adam described her in vivid detail; plus, the scenery which surrounded her. The spirit also said that she would always stay with him which meant that she was his guardian angel.

Now here's something else on medicine from the past. When we lived in our previous home, we were told to get military items from re-enactor clothing businesses which would best represent us. In addition to the clothing, I was also told to get some history books on the War of 1812.

There was even a freebee in all of this. An expensive model of a shako arrived on our doorstep from England. No one had ordered it. It was simply something my guardian angel felt we needed. When we moved, it disappeared. After we moved into our new home, Cathy and I were talking in the kitchen and it reappeared like magic right in front of us. Obviously, the shako was intended to be part of our medicine from the past.

Not all artifacts are medicine however. If an item belonged to someone else before, then you have to be aware of who the previous owner was. Your medicine and theirs shouldn't be in conflict. In other words, if you are dealing with the spirit world, then you have to know what best represents you.

# 8.6 Energy imbalances

Before a proper light fortress is in place along with the necessary crystal protection, positive energy can be depleted by spirit intruders and other external energies. For example, we give our crystals and our personal symbols extra power when we are at home. When we are away from home, there is less protective power in reserve. Because of the occasional energy imbalances in our home, a spirit intruder took advantage of a rare opportunity to possess a prized diamond ring. This is what happened.

It was Saturday and we had been out for the day as a family. Because we returned late and it was my birthday, I thought I could skip the midnight patrol for once. So we stayed up and watched a good film.

I have a unique way of detecting spirits with my sense of smell which is my main way of tracking them; so when I got up to use the washroom around four in the morning, I knew that I wasn't alone. Nevertheless, I decided to let it go until later in the day.

Later on, Cathy discovered that her mother's diamond ring had disappeared from a secure location. Because she was upset, I went upstairs with two power rods and swept the area. At the same time I requested that the ring should be returned to its original place. I went downstairs and told Cathy to go look for the ring. I stated that it should be back. Sure enough, it had been returned to its rightful owner.

After I got the ring back, I was expecting problems. Shortly thereafter, both Cathy and Jacob indicated that there was an intruder in the washroom. I opened the washroom door and pointed the two power rods point blank. Jacob said that the spirit which I had just eliminated was responsible for both the disappearing diamond ring and the washroom intrusion.

Nevertheless, disappearing items don't always come back from the spirit world on a timely basis. Our previous home was constantly in a state of imbalance, so it took over a year to get my ruby ring back. In addition, the ring had to be delivered to another address. Regardless of the circumstances, when an uncommon situation occurs during an imbalance, the universe will right the wrong in its own time.

# 8.7 How to balance energies

➤ Importance of family

- Man is a social being; so you need to find cause for celebration.

- Don't hold family grudges. Let them go instead.

➤ Increase your positive energy with the help of the spirits and protective medicine.

- Finding out what you really want to do with your life is more important than trying to be someone else. Skills can become second nature after practice; but natural strengths determine what you truly desire and how far you will be inspired to develop yourself fully; thus, creating your mission in life.

- Clues to your true purpose come from within. Nobody can tell you the truth better than yourself.

- Challenging yourself with confidence gives you more power and energy. A lack of confidence prevents you from acting on something. Confront your fears head on and be persistent. Pay attention to high levels of stress which make you feel ill at ease. Too much stress or distress probably means you're going the wrong way.

- If you hit the wall, seek solutions from your higher self. Prepare yourself to go beyond normal thinking. Remember, as you think and believe; you are. It's your ideas which make you unique.

- Turn what you want into positive energy and draw it into yourself; or use positive energy against negative energy. Putting a positive thought, against a negative thought also helps to bring balance to the universe.

- Perhaps the most important step is to act on your beliefs and really focus on what you need to do. If you believe it is something you truly desire; then you will keep your faith. That will be the true test.

- In summary: Belief ~ Ideas ~ Action ~ Results

- Finally, carry a strong mental picture of yourself, as someone who has already accomplished what you believe you should do in life.

Warning: Only use your powers for positive change.

## ➤ Spiritual transformation through awareness

Here are some key points:

- You need to step outside of power struggles; otherwise, you will make people feel insecure and it will make the problem worse.

- Anger should be controlled or avoided altogether, if confronted with evil. Express your anger in a more constructive way, by linking it with a positive strategy.

- Accept change; but don't base your life on what you see around you which is fluid and changing. It will not reflect your soul. Things which were valued a century ago are not as valued today.

Warning: Beware of false beliefs and tidings, from both the seen and the unseen worlds, if things don't seem right to you. Moreover, if you lose faith in your ability to overcome difficulties, it's possible to undo all of the success and good things that you've accomplished.

# Part Nine

## Life's Lessons

# 9.0 What I have learned

The broad road of experience means living in the material world with all the dogmas and theories which "prove" that one is right and the other is wrong. Such is the experience of religion and politics.

The road of experience must eventually lead to a narrowing of the path. Instead of looking outside for God, one needs to look at oneself and face whatever fears or doubts one has about their own true journey.

In the search for meaning, you will be tempted to take short cuts. This shows a lack of experience. It's ironic that you will only understand this truth when the time is right.

Ignorant spirits have even less opportunity to discover the truth because different levels of spiritual development are either closed or invisible to each other. By the same token, how can anyone say for sure that the New Jerusalem or a place of hell fire doesn't exist?

Padre Pio stated that he understood that the unbelievers, who deny everything which is not scientifically proven, were unwilling to subordinate their spirits or their thoughts to the higher principles of God and the supernatural. Furthermore, the unbelievers refuse to verify or discuss such matters. For them, it's much easier to dismiss the unexplainable, as unimportant.

# 9.1 Silence is the doorway to greater knowing

Here is a method which will help you with both your spiritual growth and your understanding of the paranormal. The state of not-knowing in your normal way of thinking is the doorway to true knowing. This paradox is created by going into the silence, or the state of being. This state of nothingness, of stillness and of silence is a way of creating positive energy from your thoughts and your imagination. What you identify with during the silence will change and allow you to develop with it, so that you will grow into a greater identity.

To improve your communication with your higher self, place a stone of your choice in the palm of your left hand with your right hand clasped on top. No matter what stone is chosen, we are reminded that stone is the foundation of the universe, that everything in the universe is of the same source and that the same spiritual energy flows through all things. Therefore, when we communicate with stone, we find oneness with all the living things in the universe.

# 9.2 Choosing your own path

When you're dealing with different kinds of paranormal phenomena, it's not easy to explain your experiences to others; so you stop talking about them. After you realize that most other people are not aware of any harassment issues with the spirit world on an ongoing basis, you may decide to write about your experiences instead.

Remember, it's all about the spirits. It's not about theories, or who is right or wrong, although it is safe to say that there is misleading information out there which needs to be taken with a grain of salt. No book can, or should try to explain everything that is evil and what you should do about it. As such, all that I've written is only one man's truth.

Additionally, I would say that most earthbound spirits that I've dealt with have not been attracted to me for the reasons which are mentioned in Dr. Wickland's book. Other than a few exceptions, I don't believe that the therapeutic or medical model for spirit intervention applies to me either. Nor would I say that any spirit has been turned out and tossed into someone else's aura with one wave of my mighty wand. Only those spirits that deliberately chose to harass me or someone in my family, with the intent to cause problems were exiled. Don't forget that ten to twenty years isn't very long for a spirit to be banished. On the other hand, nobody keeps their sanity for long if they are seriously haunted.

Even though I've dealt with hundreds of spirits, it wasn't my conscious choice to be a spirit tracker. It's something that was decided before my time which I have no knowledge of. My intuition is my only truth along with the word of the Creator. If I had not been audibly told by a much higher authority that I would win against these evil spirits, I would have begun to doubt my mission after reading other popular authors who spend less time writing about the negative side of the spirit world. That is why you have to choose your own path when you have no one else to turn to.

*   *   *

Here is a personal case to consider. One of the most evil acts directed at me was the threat to erase my "memory banks" during the period of time when *Ghostly Allies* was being written. I never mentioned it in the book because it seemed so unreal that I "put it out of my mind." I'm glad that I didn't give it too much thought. I was under enough stress as it was. Perhaps the spirits who threatened my spiritual existence were also trying to weaken me enough to attack the ketheric layer of my aura. According to several sources, all completed soul tasks are registered in this outer layer. According to Jacob, the spirits that I was fighting at the time were intent on following my soul's link to the Akashic Records. Since I had received the information from my young boys at the time about these vindictive devils, I had no way of knowing how serious the threat was. I actually didn't believe evil spirits were capable of erasing memory banks, even though Jacob said that their threats were real enough. I do know one thing for sure. If evil spirits are capable of erasing memory banks and past lives; then it's possible to lose everything that we've learned from our re-births. In that case, without our ghostly allies, we would be lost. Perhaps there is more at stake; then just surviving and that's why we need to be strong and believe in our allies.

Whatever I do to eliminate evil spirits, I do with the blessing of the universe because I believe that most laws in this universe which govern psychic phenomena are in favour of the healing process. Once we fully understand the universal laws in regards to the healing process, it may be possible to fully understand the nature of evil and negativity in our world.

Although my two boys had been taught specific ceremonies and rituals by the spirits, so they could deal with spirit intruders, we didn't find the ceremonies to be as effective as using crystal healing rods and jet when quick action was needed. Moreover, I believe that crystal healing rods represent a step up from candles, incense, oils, stars and crosses when it comes to removing evil spirits. However, the "step up" depends on the warrior first and foremost.

I have seen the evidence that there is always untapped power waiting for you when you need it most of all. You should understand that this additional light power is to be used for the purpose of good and it will never fail you. One side benefit of replacing negative energy with positive energy is that you are also attracting good fortune to yourself.

When you finally stop with your inner struggles, you will find the answers within. Your accomplishments will take you to your next chosen step and greater truths will be revealed. Remain positive and know that you will always be supported by the universal light force.

\*     \*     \*

Since, we are closer to the world of negative spiritual frequencies than to the higher frequencies, it's important to elevate one's thoughts words and actions to the highest levels possible when interacting with all unknown spirits.

If you should ever have a liaison with a spirit, you will probably experience a prickling sensation in your mind. If this sensation spreads to your entire body, you may have allowed for a spirit attachment.

In order to avoid an attachment in the first place, continue to maintain a strong presence amongst the spirits, utilize the universal light force to help you to raise your own conscious levels and take heed. Also, remember to modify whatever strategies that you have learned to suit yourself. Just keep it simple and keep doing it consistently.

Remember that few are chosen to be spirit fighters. Instead, be at peace and look within, for the power will guide you to what challenges still lay ahead. You consciously and subconsciously chose your experiences, so that you can learn desired lessons which will make it possible for you to advance to the next stage of spiritual development.

# Part Ten

## F.A.Q.

*I've tried to answer every possible paranormal question related to "protection from negative entities" in the main text; but other questions could be related to your money concerns. For example: How do you decide when enough is enough and it's time to move on. I've done it myself. However, if I had read this book, I might have stayed and tackled the problem instead. Hopefully, the following questions and answers will provide you with a little stimulus beyond what you already know.*

*Does the law recognize that a house is haunted?*

Yes and no. The law says that a house is stigmatized when the value of a house is, *or could be*, affected by a history of murder, suicide, ghosts, "a haunting," or other unexplained happenings.

- Except for Quebec, all places in Canada at this point in time say "caveat emptor." Let the buyer beware.
- Currently, half of the United States of America recognizes the "stigmatized property disclosure form" as being legitimate.

*In what situation do you think a house really is stigmatized?*

A house could be considered to be stigmatized if it had earthbound spirits residing in it and there was a long history of paranormal happenings going back decades. In a recent survey done in Canada, 39% of the people surveyed said that they would buy a haunted home with earthbound spirits in it.

My response to the notion of a stigmatized house is this. It's a shame that no one tried to move the spirits on in the first place. More importantly, does that mean that most people don't know what to do, if they find themselves living in a haunted house?

Perhaps there are different notions of what constitutes a "haunted place," since many people do live in haunted houses without any problem. Sometimes the ghosts co-operate and sometimes they don't. If they don't, then you either get rid of them yourself, or you move on.

On the other hand, if some tangible event took place which had extremely nasty consequences (like murder for example), then you might have a case. Personally, I wouldn't want to live in the same place where someone was murdered. I wouldn't want to live on Indian burial grounds or in a mental institution either, so some disclosure is okay.

*So when should I decide to give up and sell my home?*

➤ In the first place, fight the urge and never give up. Work on yourself and you will win. I promise you; you will win.

➤ If you decide to fight, you need to follow my second bit of advice as well. Unless you want to invite more stress into your life, you should not talk about "unexplainable spirit activities" when you are dealing with closed minds.

I had other reasons for moving besides my fight with spirits. In fact, I fought them in my second home too. I even got the feeling that the Senior Council felt that I had not gone far enough with my book Ghostly Allies.

As John Wayne said, "There are some things that a man can't ride around."

The second time I stayed and I did win.

*The final question is an ethical one (if you happen to be a ghost). Should psychic investigators go into places where they are not welcomed?*

It's just as easy to pick up an entity at your local bar, as it is at your nearest haunted fort; so psychic investigators shouldn't be put off going into places where they aren't wanted. Just be prepared to defend yourself.

Psychics and sensitive people tend to draw a lot more problems to themselves because they are considered to be more intelligent in the spirit world. There are advantages to being psychic and there are advantages to being non-psychic. As a psychic investigator, I find it is better to be less sensitive to psychic phenomena; when everyone around you is sensitive.

Enjoy your challenges on the Earth plane. Remember that everyone's path is different in this life, so some of the things I have said here may not be true for you. Adopt your own symbols for protection, believe in yourself and be well.

# Appendix I: Live your life

As you read the sacred words of live your life, you will know in your heart and soul what it is to be a light warrior. Be inspired by the words of one of the greatest light warriors of all time and live your life without fear.

Live your life

Live your life that fear of death
Can never enter your heart
Trouble no one about His religion…
Respect others in their views
And demand that they Respect yours…
Love your Life, Perfect your Life…
Beautify All things in your Life…
Seek to make your life long
And of service to your people…
Prepare a noble death song for the day
When you go over the great divide…
Always give a word or sign of salute when meeting
Or passing a friend, or even a stranger, if in a lonely place
Show respect to all people, but grovel to no one…
When you rise in the morning, give thanks for the light,
For your Life, for your Strength
Give Thanks for your Food and for the Joy of Living…
If you see no reason to give thanks…
The Fault Lies in …Yourself.

Tecumseh…Shawnee Warrior

# Appendix II: Making psychic connections

During the 1960's, Eileen Sonin was perhaps the most famous psychic in the Toronto area. In fact, Cathy's aunt and uncle became good friends with Eileen and her husband. Eileen wrote two books: Ghosts I have known (1969) and Especially ghosts (1970). The first book was mainly concerned with psychic phenomena in Britain and the second book was concerned with psychic phenomena in Canada. Eileen kept her psychic abilities to herself when she was in Britain. However, after arriving in Canada, she came out of the psychic closet. Eileen was able to get the message out about the spirit world, whereas others would not risk it. Unfortunately, she died just seven years after her second book was published.

One of the stories in the book Ghosts I have known reminded me of an incident when Cathy and I first visited England together in 1989. We had been staying up in the Lake District for two weeks; but we decided to go to Bath for our final two weeks. We had rented a car for a few days with the goal of driving to Stonehenge on a rainy day. Naturally, we got completely lost for some reason. Cathy's mother side of the family came from this area and her grandfather commanded a munitions site nearby during the Second World War. Cathy said to me that her grandfather was helping her and that we would be okay. At the time I thought it was a bit strange; but I didn't question Cathy's judgment when she sounded so sure of herself. It wasn't long before we went from "completely lost," to our arrival at Stonehenge.

# Appendix III: Paranormal incident at Fort Henry August 28, 2008

*The following paranormal incident at Fort Henry occurred during the summer of 2008. This incident suggests that sometimes people can be the "source of the problem."*

We had been visiting the fort for the past six years and the fort normally closes at 5:00pm. However, today the fort was allowed to be left open until 8:00pm. Therefore, we decided to stay later than usual.

We were observing the big guns when a young boy started to "bad mouth" the fort, since he felt it was "pointless." Then, he started to kick the 24 pound cannons and make additional negative comments.

Cathy was nearby and she got slapped for no reason. Then both Alan and Jacob witnessed the naughty boy being pushing down a set of stairs by some angry spirits.

Cathy was really fed up with it all, since she would not have been hit herself, except for the irritable, bad-mannered little boy. She left the area immediately. Then both Adam and Jacob witnessed the little boy's older brother hit the little boy because he had still "not learned to behave."

If you are a seasoned ghost tracker, you can draw your own conclusions. For example: the issue of respect towards the spirits, being the innocent by-stander and being at a particular place, at the wrong time. Moreover, if you look at the situation from the ghosts' point of view, perhaps they were a little disturbed by the change in schedule.

# Bibliography

Baker, H.A. Visions Beyond the Veil: Visions of Heaven, Angels, Satan, Hell, and the End of the Age. New Kensington, PA: Whitaker House, 2006.

Bowman, Catherine. Entities Among Us: Unseen Forces That Affect Our Daily Lives. Nevada City: Blue Dolphin Publishing, Inc., 2003.

Browne, Sylvia. Temples on the Other Side: How wisdom from beyond the veil can help you right now. New York, NY: Hay House, 2008.

Carty, Rev. Charles Mortimer. Padre Pio: The Stigmatist. Saint Paul, Minnesota: Radio Replies Press, 1952.

Crowe, Catherine. Night Side of Nature. London: T.C. Newby, 1848.

Eagle, Chokecherry Gall. Beyond the Lodge of the Sun: Inner mysteries of the Native American way. Rockport, MA: Element Books Inc., 1997.

Fisher, Joe. The Siren Call of Hungry Ghosts: A riveting investigation into channeling and spirit guides. New York, N.Y: Paraview Press, 2001.

Hilson, R.G. Ghostly Allies: A true account of the supernatural. Lincoln, NE: iUniverse, 2007.

Hilson, R.G. Ghost Tracker. West Conshohocken, PA: Spoken Books Publishing, 2008.

Hilson, R.G. Ghost Tracker II. West Conshohocken, PA: Spoken Books Publishing, 2008.

Hilson, R.G. Lessons from the Heavenly Council. West Conshohocken, PA: Spoken Books Publishing, 2008.

Hilson, R.G. Haunted Fort Niagara. West Conshohocken, PA: Spoken Books Publishing, 2007.

Hilson, R.G. The Haunted Forts and Battlefields of Niagara. West Conshohocken, PA: Spoken Books Publishing, 2006.

Peck, Scott M., M.D. People of the Lie: The hope for healing human evil. New York, NY: Simon and Schuster, Inc., 1983.

Riesinger, Theophilus. The Earling Possession Case: An exposition of the exorcism of "Mary," 1934.

Price, Harry. Poltergeist Over England. London: Country Life Ltd., 1945.

Roger, John. Psychic Protection. Los Angeles, CA: Mandeville Pres, 1997.

Sapa, Hehaka. The Secret Rites of the Sioux Indians. Paris: Payot, 1953.

Steiger, Brad. Real Ghosts, Restless Spirits and Haunted Places. Detroit: Visible Ink Press, 2003.

Twitchell, Paul. Eckankar: The key to secret worlds. San Diego, CA: Illuminated Way Press, 1969.

Vivian, Margaret. The Doorway: Dictated by a soldier who passed on forty years ago. London: Psychic book club, 1941.

Wicks, Cheryl A. (with Ed and Lorraine Warren). Ghost Tracks: What history, science, and fifty years of field research have revealed about ghosts, evil, and life after death. Indiana: Author House, 2004.

Wickland, Carl, M.D. Thirty Years Among the Dead. L.A: California National Psychological Institute, 1924.

Williams, Ben: Williams, Jean and Shoemaker, John B. The Black Hope Horror: The True Story of a Haunting. New York: William Morrow and Co. Inc., 1991.

CPSIA information can be obtained at www.ICGtesting.com
Printed in the USA
LVOW082324110912

298435LV00002B/102/P